Child
Abuse
Trauma

Interpersonal Violence:
The Practice Series

Jon R. Conte, Series Editor

Interpersonal Violence: The Practice Series is devoted to mental health, social service, and allied professionals who confront daily the problem of interpersonal violence. It is hoped that the knowledge, professional experience, and high standards of practice offered by the authors of these volumes may lead to the end of interpersonal violence.

Child Abuse Trauma

Theory and Treatment of the Lasting Effects

John N. Briere

Interpersonal Violence:
The Practice Series

SAGE Publications
International Educational and Professional Publisher
Newbury Park   London   New Delhi

For information address:

SAGE Publications, Inc.
2455 Teller Road
Newbury Park, California 91320

SAGE Publications Ltd.
6 Bonhill Street
London EC2A 4PU
United Kingdom

SAGE Publications India Pvt. Ltd.
M-32 Market
Greater Kailash I
New Delhi 110 048 India

Printed in the United States of America

Library of Congress Cataloging-in-Publication Data

Briere, John.
    Child abuse trauma : theory and treatment of the lasting effects
John N. Briere
        p.   cm.   —(Interpersonal violence: The practice series; 2)
    Includes bibliographical references.
    ISBN 0-8039-3712-1 (cloth).   — ISBN 0-8039-3713-X (pbk.)
    1. Adult child abuse victims—Rehabilitation. 2. Adult child
abuse victims—Mental health. 3. Psychotherapy. I. Title.
II. Series.
  RC569.5.C55B75   1992
  616.85'822390651—dc20   92-23606
                                                             CIP
92 93 94 95   10 9 8 7 6 5 4 3 2 1

Sage Production Editor: Judith L. Hunter

Contents

Foreword

Adult problems in self-perception and self-acceptance, relationship to others, and worldview can often be understood as the logical consequences of childhood maltreatment. This simple truth is the central message of *Child Abuse Trauma*. In this book, John Briere has done something much needed in the mental health field. He has comprehensively and eloquently made the case for recognizing that much (if not most) of what we think of as adult psychopathology actually reflects long-term reactions to child abuse. Whether the abuse suffered is sexual, physical, or psychological makes a certain difference, but it is being abused that seems to matter most. Helping adults who have suffered these experiences requires being aware of this.

This book is, among other things, an excellent reference guide. Dr. Briere summarizes and synthesizes much of the extant literature from the various streams of child abuse research. He correctly includes growing up with substance-abusing parents as a form of child abuse, since emotional abuse or neglect is almost invariably a part of this experience. He even incorporates the literature on attachment, the failure of which may be the result of psychological abuse or neglect, may predispose to other child abuse experiences, and always exacerbates the effects of child abuse.

Dr. Briere's special talent is in making sense of the internal experience of child abuse survivors. He helps us understand that much of what seems pathological is really creative, albeit ultimately dysfunctional, strategy for survival. The capacity of the child or adult to live with and surmount abuse trauma becomes a strength to be capitalized on in therapy, rather than a reflection of deficits to be corrected. Even the most disturbing behaviors have functional meaning when conceptualized in this fashion. For example, the myriad self-destructive acts or behaviors so often observed in abuse survivors turn out to be more than reflections of self-loathing. They also may be efforts to reduce and control overwhelming internal affective tension that results from remembered traumatic experiences.

It is curious that major texts on psychopathology have so seldom identified child abuse as the source of adult difficulties. It is not that childhood maltreatment is not implicated, but that it is not explicitly the focus of the various explanatory models. As Dr. Briere points out in Chapter 3 of this volume, "Nevertheless, most modern theories of nonpsychotic 'psychopathology' would not predict adult symptomatology in an individual who was well treated and nurtured during childhood." One might speculate that it is the belated recognition of the prevalence of child maltreatment in our society that accounts for this failure to make the connection. And much has been said about the powerful societal and personal forces, still in existence, that have served as obstacles to the acceptance of the reality of child abuse.

The approach to therapy described in this volume emphasizes the fact that child abuse experiences are shared by many of us and are lived with in a variety of ways. Survivors are not just "them," they are "us" as well. The distance between the therapist and the client may be simply a matter of luck at not having been badly treated as a child, or of having found a pathway to adulthood in which surviving abuse did not result in especially negative outcomes.

Patience, respect, and the ability to stand in the client's shoes thus become central ingredients of effective therapy with adult abuse survivors.

LUCY BERLINER

Preface

The intellectual world is divided into lumpers and splitters: The lumpers assemble details into a bigger picture, and the splitters carve out important distinctions and draw attention to differences. John Briere in this book is casting an influential vote on behalf of the lumpers, arguing a persuasive case in favor of the common features of child abuse trauma. In doing so, however, he is bucking a major trend in the last decade toward the "balkanization" of child abuse—dividing sexual abuse from physical abuse, incest from sexual abuse, Munchausen by proxy from everything else, and so forth.

Why has this balkanization occurred and what purpose does it serve? Increasing subdivision within the field of child abuse and neglect has a number of sources—many justifiable, some not. The decisive development in the field dates from the late 1970s, when sexual abuse first established itself as a semiautonomous specialty.

The sexual abuse problem did have its unique aspects. In contrast to previous child abuse practice focused on physical abuse, diagnosis in sexual abuse relied more on interviewing skills than on physical exams. This new problem also came with major interlinks to the criminal justice system. It was further unique in that the treatment of adult survivors was as much a focus for sexual abuse experts as the protection of young victims. And, perhaps most basically, the field rapidly became so complex that to stay abreast, professionals needed to specialize.

But the split resulted as much from generational and disciplinary forces as it did from practice considerations. The child abuse field had developed an established leadership in the 1960s and 1970s that was largely medical and tended to specialize in the diagnosis of physical abuse. The new avatars of sexual abuse, however, were younger, came from a variety of mostly nonmedical disciplines, and seemed to need turf of their own on which to develop and grow. They set up their own treatment programs, conferences, and research agendas, and developed their own constituency. For a certain time, the two fields had little connection. However, points of collaboration did grow, mostly on the initiative of the old guard, which began to incorporate more concern about sexual abuse into longstanding child abuse programs.

Nonetheless, relations between the two subfields have remained somewhat distant and uneasy. In recent years, those concerned about physical abuse have watched while publicity, funding, and research have increasingly shifted to sexual abuse. Federal funding, which once ignored the problem, now tends to favor sexual abuse. Journal articles on sexual abuse, which were rare in the 1970s, now easily outnumber all other subjects in such major journals as *Child Abuse & Neglect*. This is despite the fact that sexual abuse constitutes only about one-sixth of all child abuse reports, only half the incidence of physical abuse (Sedlak, 1991).

These are signs that the field of child abuse is developing in a lopsided, competitive way that may not be in the true interest of children. Other signs include the fact that some aspects of child abuse have yet to garner much professional attention. Emotional abuse may be the cornerstone of all abuse, yet it has received little study. Neglect is the largest portion of some child protective services (CPS) caseloads, yet it has not mustered much excitement from researchers, professionals, or the media.

The balkanization of child abuse has had some very negative consequences. Professionals in the field are not being exposed to complete, well-rounded training in all forms of child abuse. Referrals to CPS are following fads in the literature and media. Children and families are not receiving comprehensive assessments. Researchers and theorists are missing important connections.

It would seem that the time has come for a return to a broader, unified perspective on the child abuse problem, a perspective to which this book clearly points. In this effort, contributions are needed at many levels. We need leaders and organizations that will reassert the essential unity of the field of child abuse and neglect. The recent reports and recommendations of the U.S. Advisory Commission on Child Abuse and Neglect are moves in this direction, as is the foundation and growth of a new professional organization, the American Professional Society on the Abuse of Children, bringing together workers from all aspects of the field.

We also need the development and recognition of a common body of knowledge for workers in the field that includes and cuts across all aspects of the problem. It should be expected that all specialists in the field have this common generalist background. Unfortunately, this task is made difficult by the field's interdisciplinary nature and the unavailability of many truly comprehensive textbooks and training materials. But it is clearly possible.

Finally, we need more research, theory, and clinical treatises, such as this one, that adopt an integrated, holistic view of child abuse. More emphasis and discussion need to be given to the common occurrence of various kinds of abuse, to the fact that one kind of abuse can be a risk factor for another, and to the common traumagenic dynamics underlying child maltreatment.

Because of what it contributes on all of these fronts, this book is a very important catalyst toward reintegration in the field of child abuse. Just as important, however, John Briere illustrates that a step toward reintegration does not have to be a step into the past, a rehashing of the basics or a stew of abstractions and vague generalities. He reintegrates the field with new concepts, fresh insights, and a textured and detailed analysis of the trauma of child abuse. Let us hope that the 1990s will be a decade when more will come to see the field and its possibilities with a vision as broad as his.

DAVID FINKELHOR

Introduction

The mental health and social welfare fields have been undergoing a quiet—and at times not so quiet—revolution in the last several decades. Beginning with Kempe and colleagues' description of the "battered child" in 1962, followed by books on child sexual abuse in the late 1970s and the 1980s, and culminating in recent studies of the psychological maltreatment of children, clinicians are becoming increasingly aware of the millions of children who are maltreated in our society each year. Because, in the absence of appropriate intervention, hurt children often grow to become distressed and symptomatic adolescents and adults, this awareness of child maltreatment is slowly calling into question long-cherished clinical "truths" regarding the etiology and treatment of a variety of adult psychological problems and disorders.

This book addresses this revolution in mental health conceptualization and practice. In it, I summarize the known prevalence of the major forms of child abuse (psychological, physical, and sexual abuse, as well as emotional neglect and being raised by substance-addicted parents), their incidence, and their long-term impacts on older adolescents and adults. In addition, I outline the philosophy and technique of abuse-focused psychotherapy, previously presented specifically for adults molested as children (Briere, 1989), and now expanded to incorporate the treatment of other forms of long-term child abuse trauma as well.

Central theses of this book are as follows:

1. The majority of adults raised in North America, regardless of gender, age, race, ethnicity, or social class, probably experienced some level of maltreatment as children.
2. Such negative experiences, according to their severity and their interaction with other important variables such as social and familial support, external stressors, and developmental level at the time of maltreatment, can have significant impacts on later self-perception, behavior, and psychological symptomatology.
3. Despite the above, the connection between child maltreatment and later dysfunctional or "pathological" behavior has often been overlooked and/or trivialized, partially as a result of cultural acceptance of physical violence, verbal aggression, and exploitation in the training and control of children.

A final, and more optimistic, theme in this book is that extended and regular interactions with a compassionate psychotherapist—one who is guided by an accurate understanding of abuse-related psychological trauma—may allow the former child abuse victim to address her or his early injuries, and to grow beyond abuse-imposed behavior patterns and life constraints. In this area, more than in others, the absence of empirical data becomes clear: With only a few exceptions, there is no research available to the practitioner on what works and what does not in the treatment of long-term, abuse-related psychological trauma. Given this lack, I have considered my own clinical experiences and those of other abuse-specialized clinicians, along with extant research data, and attempt to present this most pragmatic of information within a broad theoretical and philosophical framework.

In order to stress the commonalities as well as differences in the long-term impacts of various types of child abuse, I present seven groups of abuse-related problems (posttraumatic stress, cognitive distortions, altered emotionality, dissociation, impaired self-reference, disturbed relatedness, and avoidance) in Chapters 2 and 3 in the context of their association with specific and combined forms of child maltreatment. As will become apparent, each form of child abuse appears to share certain impacts with other types of maltreatment, and yet can produce unique and specific psychic injuries as well.

Part III of this book is divided into a chapter on philosophy of treatment, a chapter on therapy process issues, a relatively larger chapter on general principles and techniques involved in helping survivors of childhood abuse, and a final chapter on issues often encountered in work with former abuse victims. Also included is an appendix that outlines important abuse-focused questions appropriate to the intake or diagnostic interview (the Child Maltreatment Interview Schedule).

In contrast to my own previous work and that of others, this volume restricts itself to the conduct of individual, one-to-one psychotherapy. This limitation reflects my desire to address more intensively a single treatment modality, rather than superficially surveying all forms of intervention available for abuse survivors. This narrow focus should not be interpreted as suggesting that individual psychotherapy represents the only—or even the best—intervention available for adults abused as children. The reader is referred to other sources that consider relevant group, family, marital, and self-help interventions for detailed information on such modalities (e.g., Alexander, Neimeyer, & Follette, 1991; Briere, 1989; Courtois, 1988; Dolan, 1991; Follette, 1991; Gil, 1988; J. Goodwin, 1989; Goodwin & Talwar, 1989; Maltz, 1991; Maltz & Holman, 1987; Sgroi, 1989; Trepper & Barrett, 1989).

Implicit in this book is the notion that most types of childhood maltreatment occur in the presence of other types of abuse as well, especially among those who later request clinical services. For example, it is difficult to conceive of sexual child abuse without considering the psychological abuse also present (e.g., betrayal, threats, stigmatization) and the likelihood of physical maltreatment (e.g., tissue damage arising from penetration or other violent contact, or physical beatings to ensure compliance). Thus treatment of any given form of abuse trauma must simultaneously address potential sequelae of other, concomitant sources of victimization. It is this likelihood of multiple abuse experiences and multiple abuse impacts in most psychotherapy clients that led me to develop this more generic volume on postabuse trauma and its treatment.

In order to illustrate especially important aspects of postabuse trauma, "case histories" are presented at various points in this book. In all instances, client identity has been rigorously protected, both by altering some combination of age, gender, occupation, and circumstance, and often by combining the stories of several individuals into one presentation. I have done this because even when a client gives permission for his or her story to be used, the implications of publishing such narratives remain complex. These include the continuing potential for subtle, inadvertent exploitation of the client-therapist relationship and the possibility that, at some later point, publication of such material might become unacceptable to the survivor.

This book is offered to the experienced abuse-specialized clinician, who, I hope, will find new ideas and approaches relevant to the treatment of child abuse effects, as well as to the general therapist who wants to understand and address more fully the connection between client "psychopathology" and the impacts of child maltreatment. Because we have only recently begun to study the effects of childhood abuse as they relate to subsequent distress in adulthood, the data and theories outlined in this book must be viewed as preliminary. The reader is invited to consider the ideas presented here in the spirit in which they are offered: as early reflections of a powerful new way of conceptualizing both psychological disorder and psychotherapy.

Acknowledgments

Special recognition is due to the following individuals, who were essential to the making of this book: Lucy Berliner, Jon Conte, Diana Elliott, David Finkelhor, Terry Hendrix, and Kathy Smiljanich. I would also like to gratefully acknowledge H. Richard Lamb for his consistent support of my research and writing.

I much appreciate Veronica Abney, Susan Bakota, Sandra Butler, Eliana Gil, Beth Houskamp, Vicky Pollock, Marsha Runtz, Sharon Sawatsky, Carmen Stukas-Davis, Julia Thacker, Rose Woo, and David A. Wolfe for their valuable feedback on earlier drafts of this manuscript.

Finally, I would like to thank my wife and best friend, Cheryl Lanktree, for reviewing, editing, supporting, and, ultimately, enduring this project. From such love all things are made possible.

JOHN N. BRIERE

PART I

INCIDENCE OF CHILD ABUSE

Types and Forms
of Child Maltreatment

❑ Sexual Abuse

Alanna

Alanna is a 26-year-old woman, currently a secretary at a used-car sales office, who has recently begun psychotherapy for help with "addictions and codependency." By her own account, Alanna has engaged in sexual behavior with a large number of partners, is addicted to crack cocaine and alcohol, and has been arrested on multiple occasions for shoplifting. She is currently living with a physically and sexually abusive boyfriend, for whom she occasionally works as a prostitute in order to obtain more money for his heroin habit. This relationship is quite tumultuous, and has precipitated several self-mutilation episodes and suicide attempts in the last four months. Alanna's psychiatrist has diagnosed her as having a

3

borderline personality disorder, both in light of the above history and given her intense and variable emotional responses to him during her first therapy sessions.

Alanna was continuously sexually abused by her father from age 4 to mid-adolescence, and by her oldest brother at 16. Her first experience of intercourse was at age 6 or 7, when her father's usual digital manipulation and fondling escalated to an act of violent rape. Although much of her childhood was characterized by terror and pain, the incest remained a secret because of Alanna's extreme shame and feelings of guilt, her father's threats of harm should she tell, and her desire to protect her mother from the hurt that knowledge of the incest would bring. At around age 13, Alanna began to "use" her incest to gain favors, money, and extra privileges from her father—a time, Alanna now understands, when her self-hatred began to intensify.

The prevalence of childhood sexual abuse in our society is quite high. When defined as sexual contact, ranging from fondling to intercourse, between a child in mid-adolescence or younger and a person at least five years older, the sexual victimization rate is generally considered to be around 20%-30% for females (Finkelhor, Hotaling, Lewis, & Smith, 1989; Russell, 1986; Wyatt, 1985) and around 10-15% for males (Finkelhor, 1979; Finkelhor et al., 1989)—although recent studies indicate that the male abuse rate may reach 20% in some nonclinical populations (Henschel, Briere, Magallanes, & Smiljanich, 1990).

The impacts of sexual abuse have been studied in greater detail than have those of physical or psychological abuse, and thus considerably more is known about this form of child maltreatment. Such research indicates that molestation usually begins when the child is less than 8 or 9 years old, and is perpetrated by someone in the mid-20s or older who is typically male (Finkelhor, 1979; Russell, 1986). Sexual abuse may be quite intrusive and violent, as opposed to the harmless affair sometimes assumed. In one clinical sample of 133 women with sexual abuse histories, for example, 77% had been penetrated orally, anally, or vaginally, 56% had also been abused physically, and 17% reported especially bizarre victimization, including ritualistic abuse, multiple simultaneous perpetrators, and insertion of objects (Briere, 1988). Diana Russell's (1986) study of 930 women in the general population revealed that 80% of those sexually abused as children had felt "somewhat" to "extremely" upset at the time of the abuse, and 78% reported experiencing negative long-term psychological effects.

Due in part to the negative impacts of such victimization on later mental health, recent studies of the incidence of sexual abuse in psychotherapy or psychiatric samples usually have revealed higher rates than are found in nonclinical groups. Six studies of female inpatients or outpatients report sexual abuse rates somewhere between 36% and 51% (Briere & Runtz, 1987; Bryer, Nelson, Miller, & Krol, 1987; Carlin & Ward, 1989; Chu & Dill, 1990; Craine, Henson, Colliver, & MacLean, 1988; Goodwin, Attias, McCarty, Chandler, & Romanik, in press). Finally, in a sample of randomly selected, nonpsychotic female psychiatric emergency room patients, 70% had self-reported histories of childhood sexual victimization (Briere & Zaidi, 1989).

Although it is likely that, if untreated, any form of sexual victimization in childhood increases the risk of later mental health problems (Berliner, 1991), certain aspects of sexual abuse appear to be especially associated with long-term psychological impacts. Research in this area has been far from conclusive, however, with some studies showing an effect of one abuse characteristic and others not. Some of this variability among studies may be due to the number of individuals studied (smaller studies have less statistical power to uncover significant relationships), whether the subjects are college students or psychotherapy clients, and which symptoms or problems are examined (Briere, 1992).

Given these provisos, it nevertheless appears that sexual abuse involving one or more of the following characteristics is frequently associated with greater trauma than abuse without such characteristics:

- greater duration and frequency of the abuse (e.g., Elliott & Briere, 1992)
- multiple perpetrators (e.g., Peters, 1988)
- presence of penetration or intercourse (e.g., Finkelhor et al., 1989)
- physically forced sexual contact (e.g., Fromuth, 1986)
- abuse at an earlier age (e.g., Zivney, Nash, & Hulsey, 1988)
- molestation by a perpetrator substantially older than the victim (e.g., Finkelhor, 1979)

- concurrent physical abuse (e.g., Briere & Runtz, 1989a)
- abuse involving more bizarre features (e.g., Briere, 1988)
- the victim's immediate sense of personal responsibility for the molestation (e.g., Wyatt & Newcomb, 1991)
- victim feelings of powerlessness, betrayal, and/or stigma at the time of the abuse (e.g., Henschel et al., 1990)

It is likely that some of what are thought to be sexual abuse effects are, in actuality, the combined effects of molestation, physical abuse, and/or psychological maltreatment, especially among clinical groups. Although sexual abuse effects usually remain when one controls for other forms of maltreatment (e.g., Briere & Runtz, 1990b; Swett, Surrey, & Cohen, 1990), the synergistic impacts of the various forms of child abuse must be taken quite seriously.

❏ Physical Abuse

Alex

Alex is a 28-year-old journeyman plumber who lives in a small city in the Midwest. His lover of eight months recently left him after he beat her during a drinking binge. As she left, this woman tearfully begged Alex to get professional help, stating that he was a "Jekyll and Hyde personality": quiet and loving much of the time, yet prone to sudden periods of rage, typically while under the influence of alcohol. Thus far in his life, Alex has been charged with three separate instances of assault: twice against coworkers and once against a former lover. Always a tense person, he has had several panic attacks a day since his lover left and is unable to sleep at night without alcohol. When he does sleep, he is plagued by nightmares, mostly of violent battles or of being hunted down by people who wish him harm.

Alex was the oldest of three children, all of whom were severely and repeatedly beaten by their father. As the eldest, Alex was often singled out for the worst treatment, including having his jaw fractured for "talking back one time too many times," and, on one occasion, being pushed through a picture window. A common punishment for all three children was being forced to kneel on bottle caps while repeating promises to be good, during which they were whipped with a belt. Alex was extremely frightened of his father as a child, and yet sought to please him in any way possible. As an adult, he denies blaming his father for the abuse he experienced, insisting, "All Dad did was teach me right from wrong."

In a culture where physical pain is often used by adults to alter or control children's behavior, it is difficult to determine what parental behaviors exceed a given threshold of aversiveness or social acceptability such that they would be defined by most people as physically abusive. For example, is it physical abuse if a parent strikes a child on the buttocks with an open hand? On the face? With a stick? If it is not abusive to spank a child once, is it abusive to do it twice? Three times? Over what period of time? Is a spanking that does not leave bruises or welts clearly nonabusive? Does the "reason" for the physical punishment (i.e., the extent of the child's "bad" behavior) determine whether or not the resultant spanking or beating is child abuse?

Despite such issues, it is clear that even given the social acceptability of lower-level violence against children in our culture, substantial numbers of children are more severely maltreated by their caretakers to a point where most people would consider them to be physically abused. Rosenthal (1988), for example, indicates that from 1977 to 1984 the state of Colorado identified 1,474 cases of confirmed serious child injury (e.g., brain damage, skull fractures, dislocations, internal injuries, serious burns) at the hands of parents or caretakers. On a national level, Gelles and Straus (1987) conclude from two large studies that the rate of "severe" parent-child violence (i.e., parental kicking, biting, punching, hitting or trying to hit with an object, beating, threatening with or using a gun or knife) in the United States has been approximately 11%-14% for the last decade. Such extreme maltreatment is no doubt responsible for the estimated 1,000 to 5,000 children killed by their parents each year in America (National Center on Child Abuse and Neglect, 1988).

Finally, studies of physical abuse histories in university samples (e.g., Graziano & Namaste, 1990; Henschel et al., 1990) indicate that some 10-20% of students retrospectively report parental violence leading to, at minimum, bruises or bleeding. Similarly, a recent study by Wiemers and Petretic-Jackson (1991) found that 15% of university students identified themselves as physically abused.

Most studies report a significant overlap between physically and psychologically abusive parental behavior, due in part to the near inevitability of coexisting psychological maltreatment at the hands of physically abusive caregivers. When both are present at high levels, this combination of psychological and physical aggression may be especially harmful—producing a childhood overwhelmingly characterized by punishment, engendering in the victim a chronic sense of personal badness.

❏ Psychological Abuse

Rita

Rita is a 37-year-old manager of a drugstore chain. A "workaholic," she regularly puts in 12-hour days at the office, claiming that her job minimally demands that amount of time. Her coworkers see Rita as cold, critical, and perfectionist—someone they sometimes respect for her efficiency at work, but whom they carefully avoid socially. Unknown to her staff and peers, Rita is plagued by chronic feelings of inadequacy, ill-defined guilt, and an almost overwhelming fear of failure. She is aware that people avoid her, but tells herself that she is happier that way.

Rita was raised by her maternal aunt and uncle after the accidental death of her parents when she was 4 years old. As a child and adolescent she was frequently ignored or, at best, treated with an irritated indifference to her emotional needs. When she did receive attention, it was primarily in the form of lectures or criticisms regarding her shortcomings, weaknesses, unattractiveness, and so on. Her aunt implied on numerous occasions that Rita was unwanted in their family, and that she was a major inconvenience and drain on family resources. Never told she was loved or valued as a child, Rita increasingly avoided others and drew into herself, and frequently fantasized of her future life as a successful, powerful, and beautiful woman whom all would admire.

One of the most common forms of child maltreatment, and yet often difficult to define, psychological abuse has only recently received significant public or professional attention. As noted by Hart, Germain, and Brassard (1987):

> Little effort has been devoted to research and intervention focused on psychological maltreatment primarily because available definitions and standards for determining its existence and impact are inadequate. Under these conditions, the limited resources available . . . have been devoted to forms of child abuse and neglect which are better understood. (p. 3)

The authors of the National Study of Incidence and Severity of Child Abuse and Neglect conservatively estimate that approximately 200,000 cases of unambiguous emotional maltreatment occurred in the United States at the time of their survey (National Center on Child Abuse and Neglect, 1981), whereas the American Humane Association (1981, 1984) notes that approximately 11-13% of all reported child abuse cases consist of psychological child abuse. As Hart et al. (1987) suggest, such figures are undoubtedly underestimates of the true prevalence of psychological maltreatment in our society.

For the purposes of this book, *psychological abuse* will be defined in terms of eight types of parent or caretaker behaviors, presented below. All but the eighth item were adapted from the findings of the International Conference on Psychological Abuse of Children and Youth, as described in the work of Hart et al. (1987) and Garbarino, Guttman, and Seeley (1986):

1. *Rejecting:* The child is avoided or pushed away; he or she is made to feel unworthy, unacceptable, and the like.
2. *Degrading/devaluing:* The child is criticized, stigmatized, deprived of dignity, humiliated, made to feel inferior, and so on.
3. *Terrorizing:* The child is verbally assaulted, frightened, threatened with physical or psychological harm.
4. *Isolating:* The child is deprived of social contacts beyond the family, not allowed friends, kept in a limited area for long periods of time without social interaction.

5. *Corrupting:* The child is "mis-socialized" (Garbarino et al., 1986): taught to behave in an antisocial manner, encouraged to develop socially unacceptable interests and appetites.

6. *Exploiting:* The child is taken advantage of, used to meet the needs of his or her caretakers.

7. *Denying essential stimulation, emotional responsiveness, or availability:* The child is deprived of loving, sensitive caregiving; his or her emotional and intellectual development is stifled, the child is generally ignored or neglected.

8. *Unreliable and inconsistent parenting:* Contradictory and ambivalent demands are made of the child, parental support or caregiving is inconsistent and unreliable, and familial stability is denied the child.

Several of these behaviors are not unique to psychological abuse. Corruption and exploitation, for example, are found in sexual abuse, whereas terrorizing is a major component of severe physical maltreatment, and neglect clearly involves rejection and denial of essential stimulation. Certain outside factors, such as parental substance abuse or psychiatric disturbance, may manifest in poor and inconsistent parenting, deprivation, terrorizing, or isolation. As noted by Navarre (1987) and others, psychological abuse is probably an inherent or core part of all forms of child maltreatment, since the majority of enduring effects of such behavior are on the child's psyche, and arise from one or more of the above behaviors.

Psychological maltreatment, by virtue of its ability to distort perceptions and assumptions regarding self, others, the environment, and the future, and its presence in other types of maltreatment, has broad impacts on later psychosocial functioning. It is, in this regard, an especially injurious form of child abuse (Garbarino et al., 1986).

❏ Emotional Neglect

Henry

Henry is a 43-year-old accountant who, although he denies any psychological difficulties or distress, is being seen with his wife in marital therapy. She asserts that he is a distant, unemotional man who is "just going through the motions" in their eight-month marriage. She tells the therapist that Henry doesn't know how to love and seems to fear any form of real intimacy. Henry responds that he was unaware that there were any problems in their marriage and, in fact, thought "she was getting what she wanted."

Henry was born to a 17-year-old unmarried woman who was in and out of psychiatric hospitals for most of his first five years of life, and who later committed suicide. During his mother's hospital stays he was taken care of by various members of her extended family, as well as by some of her acquaintances. Although rarely treated badly, Henry notes that he was "sort of like a package, passed around; no one really loved me too much." Seemingly unaware of the poignancy of his characterization, he describes his recollections of his mother as vague memories of "a familiar stranger who did her best and then died."

As is true of psychological abuse, emotional neglect is difficult to determine. Not only do its parameters vary according to who is defining it and in what culture it occurs (Schakel, 1987), it may also be subsumed under a more general definition of psychological maltreatment (e.g., the denial of "essential stimulation, emotional responsiveness, or availability" cited above). Despite the broad overlap between emotional neglect and psychological maltreatment, however, it is given separate attention here by virtue of the research and theory becoming available in this specific area.

For the purposes of this discussion, *emotional neglect* is defined as per Dean (1979), cited in Schakel (1987), as an

> act of omission, frequently the result of parental ignorance or indifference. As a result, the child is not given positive emotional support and stimulation. Parents may give adequate physical care to their child but leave him or her alone in a crib for long periods of time, seldom cuddle or talk to the child, or fail to give him or her encouragement and recognition. (p. 19)

Emotional neglect was probably first raised as a major issue by Rene Spitz (1945, 1946), who described the well-being (or lack thereof) of 91 young children who had been raised since birth in orphanages. These children, although receiving reasonable physical and medical attention, were rarely spoken to, played with, or interacted with in any way beyond what was minimally necessary for their physical care. Spitz found that these boys and girls were far more lethargic, malnourished, and feeble than would be expected given their physical surroundings; in fact, one-third of them died in infancy. Although Spitz referred to this phenomenon as "hospitalism," suggesting that the syndrome was related to institutional care, a number of investigators have since shown that equivalent (although usually less severe) symptoms occur in noninstitutional settings, including intact families (see, e.g., Bullard, Glasser, Hagarty, & Pivchik, 1967; Gardner, 1972). The injurious factor thus appears to be that of insufficient psychological or emotional availability of the child's primary caregiver(s), rather than the presence or absence of parents per se.

There are almost no studies available regarding the impact of childhood emotional neglect on adult psychological functioning—primarily because such maltreatment is difficult for adults to "pin down" sufficiently to report it retrospectively, and because longitudinal studies of children have not been running long enough to allow study of neglect-related symptomatology in older adolescents or adults. Recent longitudinal research has demonstrated, however, that children who are raised by unloving, unresponsive, or otherwise emotionally neglectful parents are at risk for psychological disturbance in the short and intermediate term, perhaps especially in terms of disturbed attachment to and relationships with others. Studies conducted by Egeland and colleagues (e.g., Egeland & Farber, 1984; Egeland, Sroufe, & Erickson, 1983) suggest that psychological neglect may have pervasive and severe negative effects, impacts that future research may link to equally severe outcomes in adulthood.

❑ **Parental Alcoholism
and/or Drug Addiction**

Clara

Clara is a 43-year-old ophthalmologist, married with one child, who has been in therapy for two years. Since late adolescence she has experienced bouts of mild depression and anxiety, free-floating feelings of guilt and shame, and a sense that she is "a phony, an impostor." As treatment progresses, Clara is coming to realize the extent to which she lives a double life: on one hand functioning as a competent and successful professional, on the other "secretly" responding to life events as an insecure and needy child who never quite knows what she has done wrong.

Clara's father was a physician whose alcoholism destroyed a promising academic career by his early 40s. Clara has many painful memories of her father staggering from room to room in a drunken state, of him striking her mother during violent arguments, and of times when he would tearfully demand she talk him out of suicide. By Clara's fifteenth birthday, her mother had left her father, and Clara was essentially responsible for his care. She was unable to leave home until her mid-20s, even then experiencing considerable guilt at having "abandoned" her father.

It has been estimated that at least 28 million children in the United States live in families where one or both parents are alcoholics, and that "many of these individuals suffer a variety of problems related to the alcoholism of a parent that was never labeled as such" (Brown, 1988, p. 11). The incidence and psychological impacts of parents addicted to other substances (e.g., heroin or cocaine) are less known, but are likely to be equally significant.

Although the empirical data on the long-term impacts of living with an alcoholic or drug-addicted parent are limited, the recent proliferation of adult children of alcoholics (ACA) groups and organizations, as well as growing clinical interest in the problems of such individuals, suggests that this is a significant form of child maltreatment in our society. All of the types of abuse and neglect outlined thus far in this chapter, in fact, have been linked to alcohol-intoxicated parents in the clinical and research literature (e.g., Kaplan, Pelcovitz, Salzinger, & Ganeles, 1983; Murphy et al., 1991). In addition, adults in therapy who were psychologically, physically, and/ or sexually abused as children frequently describe their maltreatment in the context of parental drunkenness or drug intoxication.

The association between alcohol abuse and child maltreatment is so common that various writers have implied that family dynamics arising from and sustaining parental alcoholism, rather than abuse per se, are the primary etiologic factors in the child's later psychological disturbance. It is likely that being raised in a family with substance-addicted parents increases the likelihood of—at minimum—psychological abuse and neglect, and should be understood by clinicians as such. It is probably not true, however, that parental alcoholism or "the alcoholic family" is necessarily the only underlying traumagenic factor in such cases, nor do all instances of child abuse occur in the context of alcohol. Instead, alcoholic behavior may represent one of several toxic phenomena simultaneously present within a given family, such that parental substance addiction and concurrent physical, psychological, or sexual abuse may have both unique and overlapping negative impacts on the child's current and future psychological functioning (Elliott & Edwards, 1991).

In the most comprehensive review and integration of the literature on adult children of alcoholics to date, Brown (1988) characterizes the alcoholic family environment as one of "chaos, inconsistency, unpredictability, unclear roles, arbitrariness, changing limits, arguments, repetitious and illogical thinking, and perhaps violence and incest. The family is dominated by the presence of alcoholism and its denial" (p. 27).

Adults who were raised in families with an alcoholic parent frequently describe a childhood filled with fears—often for themselves, other family members, and the alcoholic him- or herself. They may report times when the substance abuser was out of control, rapidly cycling from one dramatic affect or behavior to another (e.g., hilarity to rage to remorse), and seemingly dangerous to him- or herself and others. Perhaps even more significant, adult children of alcoholics were often immersed in an environment characterized by chronic unpredictability and unreliability. There is often a sense that the child was deprived of being parented—instead living with one or more people who could not be counted upon for safety, security, or nurturance. The alcoholic often forces the child into a caretaking/parental role by virtue of his or her own regression, neglectfulness, or primitive demands (Brown, 1988).

❑ Other Forms of Abuse

This chapter has outlined some of the major forms of child abuse found in our society. Other, less studied types are also quite prevalent, and clearly deserve further attention. Witnessing family violence, perhaps especially one's mother being battered by one's father, for example, is clearly abusive and has been related to subsequent psychological disturbance (Jaffe, Wolfe, & Wilson, 1990; Rosenberg, 1984). In males, exposure to parental spouse abuse during childhood has been associated with a later willingness to be violent in relationships (Briere, 1987; Stacey & Shupe, 1983). A strong case can also be made for considering social discrimination, racism, sexism, and war as, among other things, culturally supported child maltreatment (Ayalon & Van Tassel, 1987; Gil, 1987; Jones & Jones, 1987; Reschly & Graham-Clay, 1987).

Extreme poverty and homelessness exemplify ways in which American society fails to provide minimal support for many of its citizens and, as a result, indirectly maltreats large numbers of children. It is currently estimated, for example, that one in five school-aged children and one in four preschoolers are living in poverty (Molnar, Rath, & Klein, 1990). An article in the American Psychological Association's *Monitor* reported that 100,000 children in the United States currently live in families without homes, and quoted Health Commissioner Nancy Boxhill's testimony to a Senate subcommittee that "all over America, in our cities and rural areas, children are living in cars, cardboard boxes, and abandoned buildings and shelters" (Landers, 1989). The negative impacts of such living conditions have yet to be studied in detail, yet are bound to be significant (Bassuk & Rubin, 1987; Rescorla, Parker, & Stolley, 1991).

Together, these various forms of cruelty and deprivation provide a vast store of negative childhood experiences that, in turn, have significant—yet frequently overlooked—impacts on the later mental health of millions of people. As will be shown in the next two chapters, such abuse-related problems include many of the "disorders" and dysfunctional behaviors currently of major interest to clinicians.

PART II

THE LONG-TERM IMPACTS OF CHILD ABUSE INTEGRATION OF RESEARCH AND THEORY

Like other victims, abused children experience significant psychological distress and dysfunction. Unlike adults, however, they are traumatized during the most critical period of their lives: when assumptions about self, others, and the world are being formed; when their relations to their own internal states are being established; and when coping and affiliative skills are first acquired. Such posttraumatic reactions can easily have an impact upon subsequent psychological and social maturation, leading to atypical and potentially dysfunctional development. Because of these complexities, study of the psychological effects of child abuse must consider not only the immediate impacts of maltreatment but also their subsequent interference with and impacts on normal human development over the long term. In other words, the effects of child abuse are usually dynamic and interactive, as opposed to merely the expression of early trauma as it waxes and wanes over time.

Regardless of specific type of maltreatment, child abuse impacts are likely to occur in at least three stages:

1. *initial reactions to victimization,* involving posttraumatic stress, alterations in normal childhood development, painful affect, and cognitive distortions
2. *accommodation to ongoing abuse,* involving coping behaviors intended to increase safety and/or decrease pain during victimization

3. *long-term elaboration and secondary accommodation*, reflecting (a) the impacts of initial reactions and abuse-related accommodations on the individual's later psychological development and (b) the survivor's ongoing coping responses to abuse-related dysphoria

Although some of the initial reactions of victims to their abuse may abate with time, more typically such disturbances, along with abuse-specific coping behaviors, generalize and elaborate over the long term if untreated.

The following two chapters review the current literature on the long-term psychological impacts of child abuse, and integrate it with current clinical knowledge and perspective. Chapter 2 summarizes the long-term psychological impacts of child maltreatment, whereas Chapter 3 describes the various "dysfunctional" behaviors often engaged in by abuse survivors. The reader will notice that the bulk of this research deals with the problems and symptoms associated with a history of sexual abuse. As noted in Chapter 1, study of the extended impacts of emotional neglect, psychological maltreatment, parental substance addiction, and physical abuse is in its infancy, and thus definitive data in these areas are difficult to obtain. Nevertheless, the growing data base on child abuse effects allows certain tentative conclusions regarding the enduring effects of various types of maltreatment to be made, especially when the insights of abuse-specialized psychotherapists are taken into account.

Considered in the following chapters are seven major types of psychological disturbance, all of which are frequently found in adolescents and adults who were abused in childhood:

- posttraumatic stress
- cognitive distortions
- altered emotionality
- dissociation
- impaired self-reference
- disturbed relatedness
- avoidance

Also considered will be the implications of postabuse sequelae for "codependency" and "borderline personality disorder."

2

Long-Term Impacts of Child Abuse I: Psychological Responses

☐ **Posttraumatic Effects**

Alicia

Alicia presents to a psychiatric emergency room with fears of "going crazy." Currently 18 years old, she describes a four-year history of panic attacks, nightmares, "seeing bad things in my mind," sudden, unexpected thoughts about sex and/or violence, and impaired concentration. During her psychiatric interview Alicia seems quite tense, and yet describes her symptoms in a detached, almost impersonal way. Although she does not connect her childhood history to her current problems, she was raised by an alcoholic stepfather who was both sexually and physically abusive to both her and her 14-year-old sister, and who frequently evicted her from the household for a variety of minor or nonexistent transgressions. The "bad things" that Alicia occasionally "sees" are drops of blood on a linoleum floor, her father screaming at her, and "sex things" (she will not amplify on this).

The term *posttraumatic stress* refers to certain enduring psychological symptoms that reliably occur in reaction to a highly distressing, psychically disruptive event. According to DSM-III-R, a diagnosis of post-traumatic stress disorder (PTSD) requires that the following be present:

- An aversive event has transpired, of sufficient severity that it would evoke significant psychological disturbance in almost anyone.
- The event is frequently reexperienced via nightmares, intrusive thoughts, or flashbacks (sudden sensory memories that seem immediately real even though the event is long past).
- The individual experiences a "numbing of general responsiveness" to, or avoidance of, current events in his or her world.
- There are "persistent symptoms of increased arousal," such as sleep disturbance, heightened startle response, or poor concentration. Also included in this domain is "physiologic reactivity upon exposure to events that symbolize or resemble an aspect of the traumatic event" (American Psychiatric Association, 1987, pp. 250-251).

Traditionally, PTSD has been diagnosed when the above symptoms are found in victims of natural catastrophes, disasters, war experiences, or accidents. More recently, however, clinicians have increasingly applied this diagnosis to victims of interpersonal violence, such as torture, rape, physical assault, and child abuse.

Sexual child abuse has been shown to produce both immediate and long-term posttraumatic symptoms in some individuals. McLeer, Deblinger, Atkins, Foa, and Ralphe (1988), for example, report that most of their sample of sexually abused 3- to 16-year-olds met diagnostic criteria for PTSD, whereas Lindberg and Distad (1985) report that the symptoms of all 11 of the adults with incest histories in their clinical sample justified diagnoses of chronic PTSD. Similarly, Briere, Cotman, Harris, and Smiljanich (1992) report that both clinical and nonclinical groups of sexual abuse survivors report intrusive, avoidant, and arousal symptoms of PTSD on the 104-item Trauma Symptom Inventory (TSI; Briere, 1991).

Especially prominent for sexual abuse survivors are PTSD-related intrusive symptoms. The most disturbing of these, by virtue of their uncontrollability and perceived bizarreness, are flashbacks. These sudden, intrusive sensory memories often include visual images of the abuser's face or aspects of the actual sexual assault taking place, hearing the perpetrator's voice making abusive and/or obscene statements, choking sensations related to forced oral intercourse, sometimes accompanied by the taste of semen, smelling the molester's alcohol-laden breath, and feeling hands grabbing one's legs, thighs, or genitals. Such flashbacks, although sometimes seeming to occur "out of the blue," usually are triggered when the survivor comes in contact with abuse-related events or stimuli. Known triggers of flashbacks include sexual stimuli or interactions, abusive behavior by other adults, disclosure of one's abuse experiences, or reading or seeing sexual or violent media depictions (Courtois, 1988; Gelinas, 1983; Meiselman, 1990).

The sexual abuse survivor may also have repetitive, intrusive thoughts and/or memories of childhood sexual victimization, making it difficult to concentrate for extended periods, or to have a "normal" (i.e., nondistressing) mental life. Typically, intrusive thoughts center around themes of danger, humiliation, sex, guilt, and badness. Intrusive memories usually involve unexpected and unwanted recollection of specific abusive or traumatic events in seemingly unrelated contexts.

In some ways similar to flashbacks and intrusive thoughts, most adolescent and adult abuse survivors in therapy report abuse-related nightmares. These nightmares appear to be of two types: either graphically realistic renditions of the original abuse trauma (Type I) or more symbolic representations of victimization, involving themes of intrusion, violation, violence, and/or danger (Type II). Type I nightmares often appear soon after the abuse, and usually decrease in frequency over time. Type II nightmares seem to be both a short- and long-term sequel of trauma, often surpassing Type I nightmares as the survivor grows older.

Although the literature on abuse-related PTSD has addressed most frequently childhood sexual victimization, this is undoubtedly more the result of the paucity of research on the lasting effects of physical maltreatment than any differential impact of molestation per se. Clinical experience suggests that adolescents and adults with physical abuse histories quite frequently report posttraumatic symptoms during therapy. Empirical evidence for the connection between childhood physical abuse and later posttraumatic stress includes the elevated Trauma Symptom Checklist (TSC; Briere & Runtz, 1989a) and Trauma Symptom Inventory (TSI; Briere, 1991) scores of individuals who were physically maltreated as children (for reviews, see Briere et al., 1992; Elliott & Briere, 1991c), and the fact that equivalent physical assaults during adulthood also can produce PTSD (e.g., Kilpatrick et al., 1989; Saunders, Mandoki, & Kilpatrick, 1989).

The posttraumatic symptoms of physical abuse survivors appear to involve more autonomic arousal (e.g., tension, "jumpiness," flinching), avoidance of abuse-related thoughts or stimuli, violent nightmares, and intrusive thoughts of being violent or of suddenly being injured than do those produced by sexual abuse alone. Intrusive violent thoughts may be especially frightening for the former physical abuse victim, since, as a result of their suddenness and perceived uncontrollability, they seem to suggest uncontrollable aggressive impulses and, possibly, violent behavior. When flashbacks occur in physical abuse survivors, they are often triggered by the survivor's own angry or rageful feelings, overt conflict with others, violent events, or being in the presence of someone who is in some way physically frightening. Such flashbacks may be of especially grievous abuse, such as instances of injury-producing blows, torture, bondage, ritualistic maltreatment, or of times when the survivor feared or expected immediate injury or death.

PTSD as a result of childhood psychological abuse has not been reported frequently in the literature, nor is it a prominent feature in the clinical presentation of adolescents or adults whose maltreatment as children was restricted to psychological abuse. One exception, however, may be in the area of psychological abuse by "terrorizing," as described in Chapter 1, and/or of witnessing violent assaults upon others. Probably because such behaviors imply threats of actual physical abuse or violence, posttraumatic stress has been linked to terrorization in children (Pynoos & Eth, 1984; Terr, 1990) and appears to be present in some adults who were terrorized but never physically injured in childhood.

❑ Cognitive Distortions

Aaron

Aaron is a 27-year-old man who has been in intensive psychotherapy for the last three years, seeking help for pervasive feelings of insecurity, low self-esteem, fearfulness in social settings, and lack of assertiveness. As therapy has progressed, Aaron has become increasingly aware of the extent to which he silently disparages and criticizes himself—an internal monologue of disconfirmation that engenders chronic feelings of helplessness and inadequacy, both at work and in his interactions with others. Aaron reports being "frozen" by indecision and fear of failure, and of feeling like "a weak, bad, stupid person." He denies having been abused as a child, instead describing his parents as perfect. More clear to his therapist, however, is the fact that Aaron's father was a distant, perfectionist person who held impossibly high standards for his son, and who was sharply critical when Aaron failed to accomplish what was expected of him. Both of his parents reportedly prided themselves on never having physically beaten Aaron, instead (according to Aaron) having used "psychological methods of control."

Cognitive and psychodynamic theorists generally agree that people make significant assumptions about themselves, others, the environment, and the future based upon childhood learning. Because the experiences of former child abuse victims are, by definition, usually negative, these assumptions and self-perceptions are often distorted. Abuse survivors may, for example, overestimate the amount of danger or adversity in the world, and underestimate their own self-efficacy and self-worth.

As would be predicted from the above, study of the cognitive impacts of sexual violence has linked childhood molestation to subsequent guilt, low self-esteem, and self-blame (e.g., Jehu, 1988; Jehu, Gazan, & Klassen, 1984-1985), along with other dysfunctional attributions (e.g., Henschel et al., 1990; Runtz, 1987). Gold (1986), for example, found that women with a history of child sexual abuse were more likely to attribute negative events to internal, stable, and global factors, as well as to their own character and behavior. These same women tended to attribute the causes of good events to external factors. Such cognitive sequelae may contribute to or, alternatively, act as mediators of the negative symptomatology evident among adult survivors of child sexual abuse (Gold, 1986; Jehu, 1988; Runtz, 1991).

Although distorted self-perceptions have been linked to all of the major forms of child abuse, it is likely that the core or underlying basis for such cognitive disturbance is psychological maltreatment (Hart et al., 1987; Navarre, 1987). Both clinical experience and recent empirical research suggest that some of the cognitive impacts attributed to physical or sexual abuse are probably due to coexisting psychological abuse, or psychological maltreatment inherent in such abuse.

In the area of sexual abuse, Finkelhor and Browne (1985), for example, list four "traumagenic dynamics" that they feel are especially destructive: traumatic sexualization, stigmatization, betrayal, and powerlessness. As these authors note, the latter three of these dynamics are in fact cognitive; they "alter the child's cognitive and emotional orientation to the world, and create trauma by distorting a child's self-concept, worldview, and affective capacities" (p. 180). Thus, although betrayal, powerlessness, and stigmatization are integral to certain forms of sexual abuse, they are, in fact, psychological traumas arising from at least partially psychological events.

It is likely that the cognitive impacts of physical abuse are also a function of the psychologically abusive aspects of such victimization. Navarre (1987) notes:

> The assault is not (or not only) upon the physical body but upon . . .
> the individual's perception of the self as valuable . . . the individual's
> perception of the self as competent . . . [and, among other things] the
> individual's perception that the world is beneficent or neutral rather
> than innately hostile. (p. 49)

In addition to the intrinsic psychological aspects of physical abuse, physically abusive parents often justify their violent behavior toward the child by making concomitant blaming or critical statements about him or her, implying that the abuse was deserved punishment. These justifications are likely to increase the victim's sense of guilt, shame, and responsibility for the abuse, and thereby intensify the child's sense of personal badness.

The unique relationship between psychological maltreatment and negative self perceptions is suggested by a recent study that examined university women's retrospective reports of childhood sexual, physical, and psychological maltreatment as they related to three forms of psychological disturbance (Briere & Runtz, 1990b). Although results indicated that all three forms of child abuse were correlated with each type of symptomatology, more sophisticated multivariate procedures revealed, among other findings, a unique association between subjects' reports of psychological maltreatment in childhood and low self-esteem in adulthood. In other words, although poor self-image was correlated with physical and sexual child abuse, these associations were probably due to the psychological maltreatment inherent in and coexisting with such victimization.

THE DEVELOPMENT OF COGNITIVE DISTORTIONS AS A RESULT OF ABUSE

Abuse-related negative cognitions probably arise from two sources: psychological reactions to abuse-specific events and the victim's attempt to make sense of the abuse.

Abuse-Specific Responses

Perceptions of helplessness and chronic danger are thought to result from the fact that the abuse occurred when the victim was a child, and thus physically and psychologically unable to resist or defend against the abuser. Because such experiences were often chronic and ongoing, feelings of hopelessness regarding the future were also likely. Similarly, the child may have made assumptions about his or her inherent badness, based on misinterpretation of maltreatment as, in fact, punishment for unknown transgressions.

A common impact of childhood victimization is hypervigilance to danger—not only for potential physical injury, but also for psychological trauma such as betrayal, abandonment, or injustice. This expectation of injury may lead to hyperreactivity in the presence of real, potential, or imagined threats. Not only do many former victims of emotional neglect identify potential abandonment in the everyday actions of significant others, they tend to respond to such perceptions with greater emotional or behavioral intensity than others might deem appropriate. Similarly, survivors of psychological maltreatment may especially read criticism into the comments of others, and "overreact" with anger or fear. Sexual abuse survivors, on the other hand, may perceive sexual or exploitive motives in the behavior of authority figures, and respond with fearful avoidance or with compliance in the form of sexualized or passive behavior.

Compounding the child victim's sense of danger was his or her lack of defense against such threats. By virtue of lesser social status, training for obedience, smaller physical size, and lesser strength, he or she had few real options when assaulted or exploited by an adult. Resistance was often impossible or unsuccessful, and escape was, at best, typically temporary and after the fact.

The most predictable impact of this dynamic is the victim's growing assumption that he or she is without recourse or options under a widening variety of circumstances. Not only may child victims come to accept the extent to which avoidance of abuse is beyond their control, they may subsequently generalize this assumption to other, less uncontrollable, events, and respond accordingly. Chronic exposure to situations wherein one is unable to terminate powerful, aversive stimuli (e.g., beatings, forced sexual contact, continuous criticism) is thought to lead to subsequent "learned helplessness" (Seligman, 1975) and impaired self-efficacy (Peterson & Seligman, 1983).

Abuse-related learned powerlessness also may present as passivity in the face of danger and self-perceptions of inadequacy and inability to cope with aversive circumstance. As will be described in the next chapter, this sense of helplessness to stop painful or intrusive events can render the survivor especially vulnerable to revictimization later in life, and lead her or him to accept or endure dysfunctional or abusive interpersonal relationships (Runtz & Briere, 1988). Similarly, there may be a tendency for some survivors to predict negative outcomes prematurely, leading to avoidance of challenging tasks and subsequent procrastination or underachievement in school, work, or other important endeavors. This underestimation of his or her abilities and prospects may also impede the survivor's progress in psychotherapy, since he or she may assume that meaningful growth and change are impossible.

In contrast to the passivity and impaired self-efficacy noted above, other survivors of child abuse appear to deal with experiences of powerlessness through extreme investment in control (Miller, 1984). Having learned that abuse is primarily a question of who has power and who does not, some victims grow to view assertion as a primary goal of life. Survivors for whom control is a major issue may impress others as being extremely (and perhaps unnecessarily) individualistic and self-sufficient—to the point that help or support from others is viewed as intrusive or demeaning. This preoccupation with individuation and self-determination may result in isolation and alienation in contexts where intimacy and/or vulnerability are called for, including, unfortunately, sustained interactions with one's psychotherapist.

Abuse-related poor self-esteem can also result from what Finkelhor and Browne (1985) refer to as *stigmatization*—the messages that the victim directly receives from the abuser (e.g., "You deserved that." "You asked for it." "You're being punished for being bad.") or indirectly from a victim-blaming social system after the fact (e.g., "You seduced him." "Why didn't you just say no?" "What did you do to deserve it?"). This internalization of others' negative statements and judgments during or following child abuse frequently produces guilt, shame, and self-blame in adult survivors—responses that are difficult to alter short of extensive psychotherapy (Courtois, 1988).

The Abuse Dichotomy

Finally, negative self-evaluation may arise from the victim's attempts to make sense of her or his maltreatment. This process can lead to self-deprecating conclusions, including that one deserved the abuse and that one is inherently bad. The child's conclusion-forming process in this area has been described elsewhere as her or his attempts to resolve the *abuse dichotomy* (Briere, 1989).

The abuse dichotomy is hypothesized to proceed in a series of quasi-logical inferences, based on the maltreated child's understanding of the meaning of aversive parental behavior and her or his relatively primitive cognitive processes at the time (i.e., characterized by dichotomous thinking and egocentricity). This series of conclusions appears to proceed as follows:

1. I am being hurt, emotionally or physically, by a parent or other trusted adult.
2. Based on how I think about the world thus far, this injury can only be due to one of two things: Either I am bad or my parent is (the abuse dichotomy).
3. I have been taught by other adults, either at home or in school, that parents are always right, and always do things for your own good (any other alternative is very frightening). When they occasionally hurt you, it is for your own good, because you have been bad. This is called punishment.
4. Therefore, it must be my fault that I am being hurt, just as my parent says. This must be punishment. I must deserve this.
5. Therefore, I am as bad as whatever is done to me (the punishment must fit the crime: anything else suggests parental badness, which I have rejected). I am bad because I have been hurt. I have been hurt because I am bad.
6. I am hurt quite often, and/or quite deeply, therefore I must be very bad.

Together, such cognitive reactions to child abuse and attempts to draw logical conclusions from it appear to produce what initially seems illogical: passivity, self-blame, and low self-esteem as a result of being unfairly treated by another. The extent of self-hatred that these dynamics can engender is often startling, as is its endurance during treatment. The power of the abuse dichotomy for the adolescent or adult abuse survivor resides, in part, in its self-perpetuating qualities: I was (and continue to be) hurt because of my badness, and evidence of my badness is that I have been (and continue to be) hurt.

❑ **Altered Emotionality**

Donna

Donna is a sad, slightly obese 16-year-old girl who lives with her mother and maternal grandmother in her grandmother's home. She has been referred to a school counselor as a result of slowly deteriorating grades, increasing withdrawal from her schoolmates, and recent suicidal themes in her creative writing assignments. She is relatively unresponsive to the counselor's questions, answering in a monotone and as briefly as possible. When asked, she denies having any friends, hobbies, or interests, other than eating and listening to music in her room. Donna's mother reports considerable concern about her daughter, who she sees as "going downhill" for the last year or so. She links Donna's depression to sexual and verbal abuse by the girl's father until age 11, when he left the family, in combination with constant verbal fighting with her grandmother—a woman who is also sharply critical of Donna's mother. Donna's mother adds that approximately one and a half years ago Donna's father was arrested for molesting his stepdaughter from a later marriage, although the charges were ultimately dropped. Donna denies any precipitants to her depression, although she states at one point that she hates her grandmother.

DEPRESSION

Browne and Finkelhor (1986) note that "in the clinical literature, depression is the symptom most commonly reported among adults molested as children" (p. 152). They further note that two large community studies found substantially elevated rates of clinical depression in adult women molested as children, relative to their non-molested counterparts (Bagley & Ramsay, 1986; Peters, 1984). A more recent National Institute of Mental Health-sponsored investigation (the Los Angeles Epidemiologic Catchment Area Study) found an even greater lifetime risk for major depression among women molested as children (21.9%) than among those with no such history (5.5%) (Stein, Golding, Siegel, Burnham, & Sorenson, 1988). Similarly, Lanktree, Briere, and Zaidi (1991) report that a sample of child and adolescent psychiatric outpatients with sexual abuse histories were more than four times as likely to have received a diagnosis of major depression than were patients with no molestation history. These findings are supported by a wide variety of other studies documenting greater depressive symptomatology in adolescents and adults with sexual abuse histories (e.g., Briere & Woo, 1991; Elliott

& Briere, 1992; Jehu et al., 1984-1985; Lipovsky, Saunders, & Murphy, 1989).

In addition to the known association between childhood sexual abuse and later depression, several studies have demonstrated a link between physical child abuse and subsequent depressive symptoms. Elliott and Briere (1991a) found that among professional women, those with physical abuse histories rated themselves as having significantly greater depression than those with no physical abuse history. Runtz (1987), Briere and Runtz (1988a), and Henschel et al. (1990) similarly reported that three samples of university women with histories of physical abuse endorsed significantly higher levels of depression on the SCL90-R than did women with no such abuse history. Finally, Cole (1986) found that college men and women with histories of childhood physical abuse scored higher on the depression items of Briere and Runtz's (1989a) Trauma Symptom Checklist than did nonabused or sexually abused subjects.

Research on children of alcoholics also reveals increased rates of depression in older adolescents and adults. Three studies of non-clinical samples indicate that adult women who were children of alcoholics score higher on measures of depression than do their peers with nonalcoholic parents (Benson & Heller, 1987; Elliott & Briere, 1991a; Parker & Harford, 1988), one study reports that female ACAs had higher "dysthymic" scores on the Millon Clinical Multi-axial Inventory (Hibbard, 1989), and in one study female ACAs demonstrated more self-deprecation than did non-ACAs (Berkowitz & Perkins, 1988). Because of the relative infancy of such research, however, it has yet to be determined to what extent inherent and/or concomitant psychological, physical, or sexual abuse contributes to such findings. Recent research suggests, for example, that the correlation between being raised by alcoholic parents and subsequent depression is substantially reduced when one controls for concomitant abusive treatment by these parents (Elliott & Edwards, 1991).

It is likely that although sexual and physical abuse and being raised by an alcoholic can contribute to short- and long-term depression, childhood psychological maltreatment has even greater long-term impacts in this area. Clinical experience suggests that adults with childhood histories of psychological abuse are more prone to major depressive episodes and to what DSM-III-R refers to as *dys-*

thymia: a milder form of depression characterized by chronic sadness and unhappiness, low self-esteem, self-blame, and perceived helplessness.

Other than a few nonclinical studies (e.g., Briere & Runtz, 1988a; Henschel et al., 1990; Vissing, Straus, Gelles, & Harrop (1991), however, there are virtually no data available on the long-term impacts of psychological maltreatment. Nevertheless, two of the above investigations report elevated depression scores among adults psychologically abused as children.

Perhaps most relevant to the importance of psychological abuse in the genesis of depression is the work of theorists such as Beck (1967, 1976) who link dysphoric mood to negative cognitions developed during childhood. Unfortunately, cognitive theorists rarely hypothesize the conditions under which such childhood depressive cognitions might develop. Jehu (1988) has shown, however, that childhood sexual abuse is associated with a variety of abuse-related negative thoughts and beliefs (e.g., "I am worthless and bad," "I am inferior to others because I did not have normal experiences") that, in turn, are associated with later depressive symptoms. The potential centrality of psychological abuse in the development of depression-producing cognitions seemingly rests on the chronicity and specificity of such maltreatment. Being repetitively told as a child that one is "stupid" or a bad person, for example, would appear to be an especially efficient path to the development of later self-derogatory and depressive cognitions. Certainly, many clinicians report having clients in their caseloads whose dysphoric moods and self-negating thoughts appear to reflect directly their psychological maltreatment in childhood, often in the absence of any identifiable physical or sexual abuse history.

The potential long-term effects of emotional neglect vis-à-vis depression are less known than those of psychological abuse, although a few data exist on shorter-term impacts. More than 45 years ago, Spitz (1946) described a form of depression in infants who had been separated from their mothers following hospital admission. He referred to the apathy, withdrawal, lack of interpersonal responsiveness, and visible sadness of these children as "anaclitic depression," and suggested that it was the absence of maternal nurturance and contact that produced such severe dysphoria. More recent

longitudinal research by Egeland and colleagues further supports
the connection between early emotional neglect and immediate and
longer-term depressive mood (e.g., Egeland & Sroufe, 1981; Egeland,
Sroufe, & Erickson, 1983; Erickson, Egeland, & Pianta, 1989). Because the children studied by this group are still quite young, however, formal assessment with depression measures has yet to be done.
Nevertheless, Egeland (1989) notes that those children whose mothers were psychologically unavailable currently appear depressed,
socially withdrawn, and highly dependent—symptoms that suggest a
potential for depressive disorders as this emotionally neglected
cohort matures.

ANXIETY

Because child abuse is, by its nature, threatening and disruptive,
it should not be surprising that victims of such maltreatment are
prone to feelings of fearfulness or anxiety, even well after the abuse
has transpired. Interestingly, there are few data to suggest that more
obviously life-threatening abuse (such as physical attacks) is associated with greater or more enduring anxiety than those forms of
maltreatment sometimes seen as less dangerous (e.g., sexual molestation or emotional neglect). Some of the frightening qualities of child
abuse may reside in the implications it has for the child regarding
general vulnerability and susceptibility to violation, regardless of
how dangerous the event may be perceived to be by another person.
At this level, the child's subjective experience of any form of maltreatment may be associated with perceptions of danger, or even, in
some cases, fear of impending death (Conte, Briere, & Sexton, 1989a).

Abuse may also interfere with the child's developing sense of
security and belief in a safe, just world. Work by Bowlby (1973, 1980,
1982, 1988) and Ainsworth (1985), in what is generally referred to as
the "attachment" literature, suggests that early childhood experience has significant impacts on later emotional and interpersonal
development. It is thought that early parental support, nurturance,
consistency, and responsiveness produce a secure attachment between parent and infant, such that the child is able to "approach the
world with confidence and, when faced with potentially alarming
situations, is likely to tackle them effectively or to seek help in doing

so" (Bowlby, 1973, p. 208). In contrast, early parental neglect, ambivalence, inconsistency, or frank maltreatment is likely to disrupt or prevent an optimal parent-child connection, leading the child to distrust or fear parental contact, and yet often feel abandoned without it. Such infants exhibit insecure or anxious attachment: They can become extremely upset upon separation from their primary caretakers, yet may respond with avoidance, anger, or further distress upon reunion with those caretakers. A number of studies of maltreated children indicate that early abuse frequently produces anxious attachment and, as a result, fearfulness and frustration (Egeland & Erickson, 1987; Lamb, Gaensbauer, Malkin, & Schultz, 1985; Schneider-Rosen & Cicchetti, 1984).

Although some theorists relate anxiety symptoms in adolescents and adults to how attachment issues emerge and are resolved in the first several years of life, abuse-specific problems in attachment are not the only predictors of later abuse-related anxiety or tearfulness. Although early insecure attachment might pave the way for a child's especially anxious responses to later childhood trauma, it is also very likely that securely attached children who are later maltreated can also develop anxious symptoms or disorders.

In addition to the frequent presence of posttraumatic stress symptoms in abused children, elevated anxiety has been documented in older child victims of various forms of maltreatment (e.g., Gomes-Schwartz, Horowitz, & Cardarelli, 1990; Kolko, Moser, & Weldy, 1988), as well as in adults who were abused as children (e.g., Briere & Runtz, 1988a, 1988b; Hartman, Finn, & Leon, 1987; Swett et al., 1990).

Clinical experience suggests that adults and adolescents with childhood histories of abuse frequently present with cognitive, classically conditioned, and somatic components of anxiety. As would be predicted by Beck and Emery's (1985) cognitive model of anxiety disorder, abuse-related anxiety seems typically to involve the following:

- hypervigilance to danger in the environment, whether objectively warranted or not
- preoccupation with control, with the belief that even a slight loss of self-determination or self-protection could lead to danger or catastrophe
- misinterpretation of objectively neutral or positive interpersonal stimuli as evidence of threat or danger

The conditioned components of adult abuse-related anxiety reside in the fact that child abuse usually takes place in the copresence of human relationship and closeness, and, yet, intrusion, abandonment, devaluation, and/or pain. As a result, the child or adolescent abuse victim may form a classically conditioned association between various social or environmental stimuli and danger, so that a variety of otherwise relatively neutral interpersonal events stimulate fear. For example, the formerly abused adult may become anxious in the presence of intimate or close relationships, especially fearful of evaluation, or frightened when interacting with authority figures.

Perhaps the most obvious example of conditioned, abuse-related fear is that of sexual dysfunction, especially in the case of the sexual abuse survivor. Because childhood sexual molestation is likely to condition an association between sexual stimuli and invasion or pain, many adults molested as children report fear or anxiety-related difficulties during sexual contact, including reduced sexual arousal, erectile dysfunction or lubrication problems, extreme muscle tension, frightening flashbacks, vaginismus, and pain upon intercourse. Meiselman (1978), for example, reported that 87% of her clinical sample of adults molested as children had "serious" sexual problems, as opposed to 20% of those without sexual abuse histories. Similarly, in their excellent book on incest and sexuality, Maltz and Holman (1987) state that more than half of the incest survivors they studied reported pain during intercourse, and nearly as many were anorgasmic. A number of other studies also report an empirical connection between childhood sexual abuse and sexual problems in adolescence or adulthood (e.g., Becker, Skinner, Abel, & Treacy, 1982; Elliott & Briere, 1992; Jehu et al., 1984-1985).

Other than studies by Cole (1986) and Gil (1988) showing greater sexual dysfunction among physical abuse survivors, however, there are almost no data available on the relationship between nonsexual child abuse and later sexual problems. Clinical experience nevertheless suggests that although sexual abuse is probably the primary abuse-related factor in the development of adult sexual dysfunction, adults physically or psychologically maltreated as children may also report sexual problems, frequently as a result of performance anxiety, sex-related guilt, or fear of closeness or intimacy.

Somatic components of abuse-related anxiety involve the impacts of sustained fearfulness or autonomic arousal on the survivor's physical body, as well as ways in which anxiety becomes translated into excessive bodily concerns. Such problems are often referred to as *psychosomatic* or *somatization*, suggesting the interface between psychological distress and physical health. Physical problems that have been associated with child abuse histories include headaches, stomach pain, nausea, sleep disturbance, anorexia, asthma, shortness of breath, chronic muscle tension, muscle spasms, elevated blood pressure, and other physical complaints without known biological cause (e.g., Cunningham, Pearce, & Pearce, 1988; Morrison, 1989; Springs & Friedrich, 1992). Several researchers have shown a specific link between chronic pelvic pain in women and childhood sexual abuse histories (Cunningham et al., 1988; Walker et al., 1988), although Lanktree, Briere, Henschel, Morlan-Magallanes, and Smiljanich (1990) present data implicating other forms of child abuse histories in pelvic pain as well.

The psychosomatic data presented above suggest that the basis of some proportion of medical complaints presented to physicians and other health care practitioners may be less a reflection of inherent bodily dysfunction than what Derogatis, Lipman, Rickels, Ulenhuth, and Covi (1974) refer to as "the somatic equivalents of anxiety" (p. 4), which, in turn, may arise from unresolved childhood maltreatment experiences. Although researchers in the area of psychosomatic illness have essentially overlooked child abuse as an etiologic factor, it is likely that study in this area would yield important insights into the psychological genesis of certain forms of physical distress or disorder.

❑ Dissociation

Wendy

Wendy is an 18-year-old woman who has been in therapy for 14 months. Initially describing long blanks in her memory of childhood and early adolescence, Wendy was unaware of any history of sexual or physical abuse at the time of her intake interview. Her presenting complaints, however, seemed highly suggestive of a molestation history: alcohol and drug abuse since age 11, episodes of cutting her upper arms with shards of glass, and periods of indiscriminate sexual activity that resulted in pregnancies and abortions at ages 15 and 17. As therapy progresses, Wendy is beginning to recover previously dissociated memories of ongoing sexual victimization very early in life (perhaps at ages 3 to 4) by a female babysitter, and, most recently, sexual molestation by a priest during her early teens. With the emergence of each memory fragment or image into awareness, Wendy experiences intense anxiety, disgust, and almost manic periods of hyperactivity. During these times her self-mutilation increases and her use of alcohol becomes especially problematic. Although Wendy appears highly motivated to explore her trauma, she is also having increasing difficulty concentrating and frequently finds herself "spacing out" during critical points in her treatment.

Dissociation is defined in DSM-III-R as

> a disturbance or alteration in the normally integrative functions of identity, memory, or consciousness. The disturbance or alteration may be sudden or gradual, and transient or chronic. If it occurs primarily in identity, the person's customary identity is temporarily forgotten, and a new identity may be assumed or imposed . . . , or the customary feeling of one's own reality is lost and is replaced by a feeling of unreality. . . . If the disturbance occurs primarily in memory, important personal events cannot be recalled. (American Psychiatric Association, 1987, p. 289)

In a similar vein, West (1967) describes dissociation as the result of "a discernible alteration in a person's thoughts, feelings, or actions, so that for a period of time certain information is not associated with other information as it normally or logically would be" (p. 890). For the purposes of the current discussion, dissociation is defined as *a defensive disruption in the normally occurring connections among feelings, thoughts, behavior, and memories, consciously or unconsciously invoked in order to reduce psychological distress*, much as suggested by Braun's (1988) BASK (behavior, affect, sensation, knowledge) model.

Although the etiology of dissociative symptomatology is undoubtedly complex, a number of writers and researchers relate the onset of such behaviors to psychologically traumatic events, most notably trauma that occurred in childhood (Kluft, 1985; Putnam, 1989; van der Kolk, 1987). Recent studies especially have linked dissociative phenomena to childhood sexual abuse, directly or indirectly suggesting that molestation may motivate the development of dissociative states as a defense against posttraumatic distress (Briere & Runtz, 1990a; Chu & Dill, 1990; Sanders & Giolas, 1991). Other studies have implicated childhood physical abuse as well (e.g., Briere et al., 1992; Chu & Dill, 1990; Sanders & Giolas, 1991), and at least two investigations have found a relationship to psychological child maltreatment (Briere & Runtz, 1988a; Sanders & Giolas, 1991).

Putnam (1989) suggests that dissociation may serve a number of purposes for the trauma victim: "(1) escape from the constraints of reality; (2) containment of traumatic memories and affects outside of normal conscious awareness; (3) alteration or detachment of sense of self (so that the trauma happens to someone else or to a depersonalized self); and (4) analgesia" (p. 53). These dissociative activities ultimately involve a trade-off: The victim sacrifices fully integrated functioning in order to lessen the sometimes overwhelming anxiety and pain associated with complete awareness of traumatic events.

One may envision three types of dissociative behaviors that relate specifically to alterations in thoughts, feelings, or awareness, each of which is quite common among abuse survivors: disengagement, detachment/numbing, and observation (Briere, 1989).

DISENGAGEMENT

Probably the simplest and most common form of dissociation, disengagement involves a cognitive separation of the individual from his or her environment at times of stress or trauma. Often described as "spacing out" by child abuse survivors, this dissociative behavior consists of withdrawal into a state of affective and cognitive neutrality, where thoughts and awareness of external events are, in a sense, placed on hold. Most periods of disengagement are relatively brief, ranging from seconds to several minutes, and the depth of dissociation is usually quite shallow. These "time-out" periods, although sometimes volitional, frequently occur without conscious intent. In the latter case, the individual may be surprised to hear from others that he or she is inattentive during discussions or other interpersonal interactions.

DETACHMENT/NUMBING

This term refers to instances when the dissociating person attenuates the intensity of negative feelings associated with certain thoughts, memories, or ongoing events, so that she or he can engage in necessary activities without being distracted or immobilized by psychological pain. In its chronic form, this numbing process may result in an individual who is psychologically removed from her or his feelings and who may, in fact, be relatively unaware of feelings per se. When it occurs more acutely, detachment may present as a sudden loss of reactivity to internal or external events that otherwise would produce distress or dysphoria. Although not usually considered as such, it is likely that intellectualization—a defense involving excessive, analytic preoccupation with the nonemotional characteristics of threatening events—is a form of dissociative detachment. As many therapists will note, detachment and numbing are commonly invoked by survivors during psychotherapy sessions, usually as a defense against fully experiencing the pain associated with recounting painful childhood memories.

OBSERVATION

Finally, dissociation referred to as *observation* occurs when traumatized individuals experience themselves as watching (as opposed to participating in) events in which they are directly involved. In its acute form, observation has much in common with the depersonalization and out-of-body experiences found in many PTSD sufferers. Chronic observation, however, usually presents as an ingrained tendency to avoid the direct experience of stressful or traumatic events. Abuse survivors utilizing this dissociative pattern will frequently describe a feeling of calm that can be traced to a sense of being "outside looking in" and therefore not directly threatened by potentially frightening or aversive stimuli.

More severe forms of dissociation, often involving alterations in memory and behavior, are also found among adolescents and adults with childhood histories of abuse. Most prominent among these are amnesia and multiple personality disorder (MPD).

AMNESIA

Probably least studied of abuse-related dissociative phenomena, psychogenic amnesia (or repression) occurs when an individual unconsciously avoids anxiety and distress arising from painful memories by banishing them from awareness. Amnesia is especially difficult to examine in treatment or research because people engaging in this defense are, by definition, unaware of doing so. Although Freud (1966) primarily conceptualized amnesia (what he referred to as *repression*) as a primitive way of avoiding deep-seated psychological conflicts, recent research on sexual abuse survivors suggests that it is trauma, rather than conflict per se, that is more likely to motivate amnesia for distressing events. Specifically, two research groups report that 60% and 64%, respectively, of clinical sexual abuse survivor samples reported incomplete or total absence of abuse-specific memories at some point after their childhood victimization, and that such repression was predicted by the relative extent of violence present in the abuse (Briere & Conte, in press; Herman & Schatzow, 1987). The Briere and Conte (in press) study of approximately 500 sexual abuse survivors in therapy, for example, found that those reporting previous amnesia had been molested at an earlier age, had been victimized by more perpetrators, were more likely to have been physically injured as a result of the abuse, and more often reported having been fearful for their lives than those survivors without known amnestic periods. They were not, however, more likely to report especially conflictual aspects of abuse, such as sexual enjoyment or acceptance of gifts or bribes.

Although there are no published studies that describe amnesia in individuals who were physically abused as children, it is the experience of abuse-specialized clinicians and those who work with multiple personality disorder that extreme physical maltreatment (e.g., torture, severe beatings) in childhood can be repressed as well, and that physically abused adults in therapy may recover these memories much in the same manner as do sexual abuse survivors. Support for the relationship between nonsexual traumas and repression may be found in the dissociative defenses of adult soldiers in wartime, who have been shown to experience a significant amount of combat-specific amnesia (Archibald & Tuddenham, 1965; Grinker & Spiegel, 1945; Kolb, 1984), often after especially stressful or violent events (Henderson & Moore, 1944; Sargant & Slater, 1941).

The potential commonness of abuse-related amnesia in adolescents and adults has obvious clinical implications. It is likely that some proportion of psychotherapy clients who deny a history of child abuse are, nevertheless, suffering from postabuse trauma (Blake-White & Kline, 1985; Courtois, 1988, in press). Such amnesia may not resolve without considerable work on the part of client and therapist—as van der Kolk and Kadish (1987) note, "After intense efforts to ward off reliving the trauma, a therapist cannot expect that the resistances to remembering will suddenly melt away" (p. 187).

MULTIPLE PERSONALITY DISORDER

This extreme form of dissociation is defined by DSM-III-R as follows:

> A. The existence within the individual of two or more distinct personalities or personality states (each with its own relatively enduring pattern of perceiving, relating to and thinking about the environment and one's self).
>
> B. Each of these personality states at some time, and recurrently, takes full control of the individual's behavior. (American Psychiatric Association, 1987, p. 106)

Once thought to be extremely rare, MPD is now viewed by specialists in the area as considerably less uncommon; current estimates suggest that there may be many thousands of individuals suffering from this dissociative disturbance in North America (e.g., Bliss &

Jeppsen, 1985; Ross, Anderson, Fleisher, & Norton, 1991). Less controversial than MPD prevalence is its probable etiology. Most investigations in this area indicate that MPD is highly associated with a history of childhood trauma. In their oft-cited NIMH study, Putnam, Guroff, Silberman, Barban, and Post (1986) report that more than 80% and 70%, respectively, of 100 individuals satisfying criteria for multiple personality disorder had been sexually or physically abused as children. Coons and Milstead (1984) found 75% and 50%, respectively, in their sample of MPD patients. Most recently, in a multisite study, Ross et al. (1990) found that of 102 patients with multiple personality disorder, 90% had histories of childhood sexual abuse and 82% had physical abuse histories.

Putnam (1989) vividly describes the nature of such maltreatment:

> I am struck by the quality of extreme sadism that is frequently reported by most MPD victims. Bondage situations; the insertion of a variety of instruments into vagina, mouth, and anus; and various forms of physical and sexual torture are common reports. . . . After one has worked with a number of MPD patients, it becomes obvious that severe, sustained, and repetitive child sexual abuse is a major element in the creation of MPD. (p. 49)[1]

Together, the various forms of dissociation described above offer the abuse survivor a protective shield from complete awareness, and thus from the posttraumatic pain that otherwise would follow. Unfortunately, dissociation also has a downside: decreased awareness and disintegrated functioning. As a result, what was once adaptive becomes, at least in part, an uncontrollable symptom.

The implications of this partitioning of awareness for treatment are significant. There is often a dynamic tension between the survivor's need for defensive dissociation and his or her pursuit of psychotherapy. As noted in the upcoming treatment chapters, the primary goal of abuse-specific therapy is integration: the simultaneous awareness of thought, feeling, and action, of "contradictory" ego states. Dissociation, however, is equally specific in its drive for disintegration. The resultant conflict—both within the client and between client and therapist—centers around "knowing" versus "not knowing" about painful things. As a result, dissociation is frequently present during the earlier stages of abuse-focused treatment, as the survivor's tolerance for painful material waxes and wanes.

❑ Impaired Self-Reference

Amelia

Amelia is a 34-year-old woman who was emotionally neglected by her substance-dependent mother in infancy, and both sexually and physically abused by various foster parents from age 3 to 17. She has been in and out of psychotherapy since age 13, and has been seeing her current therapist for about one year. Among the issues that she is addressing in therapy are her deep sense of emptiness and dread of being alone. Especially of concern for Amelia is her seemingly instant dependency in relationships, such that any hint of rejection or abandonment by a friend or sexual partner results in angry, panicked outbursts and, occasionally, suicidal threats or attempts. Several of the women with whom she has become involved have been psychologically, physically, and/or sexually abusive to her, yet such behavior seems to increase her dependency rather than drive her away. In treatment Amelia has considerable difficulty with therapeutic boundaries; she frequently presses for intimate details of the therapist's personal life, suggests that they have a romantic relationship or at least a friendship outside of therapy, and often calls her answering service in the middle of the night for what turn out to be nonemergencies.

The abuse effects presented thus far, although speculative, nevertheless derive from a body of empirical, relatively unequivocal research. The concept of impaired self-reference, however, rests more centrally on ill-defined, yet seemingly undeniable, clinical phenomena. It is the impression of many clinicians who work with survivors of early and/or severe child abuse that such individuals often suffer from difficulties in how they relate to self (Briere, 1989; Cole & Putnam, 1992; Courtois, 1988; McCann & Pearlman, 1990), although empirical research in this area is only beginning (Briere et al., 1992;

Elliott & Gabrielson-Cabush, 1990). What "self" is, however, has yet to be clearly determined, even among object relations and self psychology theorists who see dynamics involving this construct as critical to psychological health (Hamilton, 1988). As noted by Stern (1985):

> While no one can agree on exactly what the self is, as adults we still have a very real sense of self that permeates daily social experience. It arises in many forms. There is the sense of a self that is a single, distinct, integrated body; there is the agent of actions, the experiencer of feelings, the maker of intentions, the architect of plans. (pp. 5-6)

The development of a sense of self is widely understood to be one of the earliest tasks confronted by the infant and young child (Alexander, 1992; Bowlby, 1988; Cole & Putnam, 1992). Because this process undoubtedly unfolds in the context of attachment and the internalization of important others' perceptions and expectations, how the child is treated early in life is bound to influence his or her growing self-awareness. One aspect of this problem, negative self-evaluation, was described earlier in this chapter. Perhaps an even more critical issue, however, is the likelihood that severe child maltreatment may interfere with the child's *access* to a sense of self— whether or not she or he can refer to, and operate from, an internal awareness of personal existence that is stable across contexts, experiences, and affects.

Without such an internal base, the survivor is prone to identity confusion, boundary issues, and feelings of personal emptiness. There is often an inability to soothe or comfort oneself adequately, leading to what appear to be overreactions to stress or painful affects. This impairment can also cause difficulties in separating self from others. The abuse survivor may have problems understanding or relating to others independent of his or her own experiences or needs (Elliott & Gabrielson-Cabush, 1990), or, on the other hand, may not be able to perceive or experience his or her own internal states independent of the reactions or demands of others (Briere, 1989). Such boundary problems are frequently found among adolescents and adults severely abused as young children, and are associated with a wide variety of subsequent psychosocial difficulties, including revictimization, sexual or intimacy disturbance, and, for some survivors, likelihood of victimizing others through role-inappropriate behavior.

The childhood events that lessen self-relatedness have been long discussed in the object relations literature, with authorities such as Masterson (1976), Kohut (1971), and Kernberg (1976) often voicing major points of disagreement. Most commonly, however, dysfunctional maternal behavior is implicated in the child's development of poor or negative internal self-representation. Such mothers are often depicted as actively, often unconsciously, punishing their children's attempts to separate and individuate, thereby producing offspring who cannot differentiate their internal states and needs from those of important others (Mahler, Pine, & Bergman, 1975). Although excessive demands for dependency and punishment of autonomy undoubtedly can have negative impacts on children's self-development, it is unlikely that this maltreatment is the sole source of impaired self-reference. The position offered in this book is that sustained and early childhood trauma, arising from a variety of forms of child abuse or neglect, can produce long-standing dysfunctions of self. The injurious components of such trauma are hypothesized to reside in three domains: attachment difficulties, training for other-directedness, and the impacts of dissociation on early development.

The relationship between insecure attachment and later psychosocial dysfunction is described in Chapter 3, primarily in terms of intimacy and relationship problems. At the most basic level, parental neglect or punitive response to the infant's attachment needs may deprive him or her of an "internal working model of self" (Bowlby, 1988) in the context of the interpersonal environment. As Putnam (1990) notes, the development of self is ultimately a social phenomenon, wherein the growing child internalizes the perceptions and expectations of others, and defines his or her identity in terms of a growing differentiation from his or her caretakers. In the presence of parental emotional neglect, inconsistency, or more blatant maltreatment, however, this crucial input is lacking or distorted, as is the secure loving base from which the luckier child can explore the world and progressively surmount surmountable obstacles. As Reiker and Carmen (1986) put it, "Ultimately, these children are deprived of the experience of separateness and of any sense of their own value in being separate" (p. 364).

The attachment difficulties of the neglected or abused child may thus translate into a continuing inability to define oneself in contradistinction to the needs or views of others in the interpersonal environment. As a result, the poorly attached child may be prone to a hungry overreliance on others to define self, with associated fears of personal annihilation in the presence of abandonment, or a tendency to avoid others and exist in a semiautistic interpersonal vacuum where fewer interpersonal anchors are required or depended upon. Such basic difficulties in self-regulation may, in turn, alter or exacerbate the impacts of other, later abusive experiences (Alexander, 1992).

Although attachment dynamics are most prominent in the first several years of life, it is quite likely that later developmental events also have impacts on the solidification of identity and self-awareness (e.g., Bowlby, 1988; Putnam, 1990). This broad window of vulnerability means that experiences of maltreatment during childhood can produce not only cognitive, affective, and posttraumatic symptoms, but also dysfunctional self-perceptions and impaired self-reference.

Equally relevant to self-reference difficulties is what has been described elsewhere as *other-directedness* (Briere, 1989). This concept refers to the fact that many survivors of severe child abuse experienced invasion, exploitation, sudden and unpredictable violence, and betrayal or abandonment during large portions of childhood and adolescence. As noted earlier, the abuse victim quickly learns that safety is predicated upon hypervigilance. She or he may become adept at reading the slightest nuance in the abuser's demeanor or behavior, since rapid and accurate assessment of that person's psychological or emotional state may allow the victim either to avoid an abuse episode or to placate/satisfy the perpetrator before a more aversive event transpires. The child's proficiency at meeting the needs and/or avoiding the violence of the abuser, however, exacts a psychological price: The sustained attention she or he must pay to environmental threats inevitably pulls energy and focus away from the developmental task of self-awareness. At a time when loved and well-treated children are becoming acquainted with self—celebrating a developing sense of discovery, autonomy, and fledgling impressions of self-efficacy—the abuse victim is absorbed in the daily task of psychological and physical survival.

Thus the defensive requirement of other-directedness implies an equivalent lack of self-awareness. As a result, the survivor may be exquisitely attuned to the experience of others, but relatively unaware of his or her own needs, issues, or dynamics. Such individuals have a difficult time moving beyond a reactive survival mode later in life, and experience considerable difficulties at times when self-awareness, self-soothing, and self-confidence are called for.

A final abuse-related contribution to impaired self-reference is that of early dissociation. As previously noted, traumatized children and adults frequently deal with painful experiences, memories, and feelings by somehow altering conscious awareness, whether this be amnesia for hurtful events, numbing of anxiety, or encapsulation of trauma in the form of multiple personalities. Such defensive behaviors are often immediately adaptive, but may ultimately result in serious difficulties for the abuse survivor—especially if such dissociation begins early in life (Briere & Conte, in press). Given what has been said in this chapter regarding the development of self during childhood, it follows that any phenomenon that alters ongoing conscious awareness during this critical period is likely to have an impact on the child's sense of coherent "me"ness. The presence of depersonalization, derealization, compartmentalization, and so on may produce splits or shifting boundaries in the child's sense of self—a fragmentation that, given the role of self as an organizing entity, is likely to persist and elaborate into adolescence and adulthood. Thus, for example, a child whose sense of self includes discontinuous memories of childhood, whose identity is variable according to outside experience, or whose affective experience fluctuates as a result of intrusive or avoidant symptomatology is unlikely to develop a stable point of reference or home base from which to address the world. In the words of one angry (but articulate) adolescent survivor: "Don't you understand? There's nobody inside here to hear what you say. I'm just empty. I just do what happens" (Briere, 1989, p. 47).

The effects of child abuse presented thus far have in common their primary impacts on the survivor's inner experience, as opposed to his or her behavior in the outside world. The next chapter addresses a related, more visible aspect of postabuse trauma: the various "dys-functional" or seemingly self-defeating behaviors engaged in by some child abuse survivors. The adaptive aspects of these behaviors will be examined, based in part on their ability to disrupt or modulate the aversive internal experiences outlined in this chapter.

❑ Note

1. Because of the complexity inherent in the treatment of multiple personality disorder, both in terms of its clinical presentation and the specialized techniques used in its resolution, this topic requires far more in-depth coverage than is possible in this volume. The reader is referred to the several books available on the assessment and treatment of multiple personality disorder, especially texts by Kluft (1985), Putnam (1989), and Ross (1989).

3

Long-Term Impacts
of Child Abuse II:
Behaviors and Relationships

The psychosocial sequelae of child abuse often receive greater attention from clinicians and researchers than do those difficulties outlined in Chapter 2. These behavioral impacts of child abuse are more
likely to make problems for—and focus the attention of—the mental
health and criminal justice systems than are internalized sequelae.
Although this special attention to "problem" behavior inaccurately
suggests that the suffering of the depressed, withdrawn, or dissociated survivor is somehow less significant, work in this area is nevertheless of great importance in terms of its implications for the prevention of a wide variety of societal ills. Extrapolating from the
research of Widom (1989), Pollock et al. (1990), and McCord (1983), for
example, it is likely that society's problems with drug addiction,
alcoholism, violent crime, and suicide would be reduced substantially if child abuse were prevented and/or successfully treated.

The external manifestations of child abuse are not all readily calculated by studies of police blotters or social service rosters, however. Many abuse survivors experience difficulties in less visible social domains, such as their relationships with important others. As discussed below, adults who were abused or neglected as children often have difficulties with intimacy, trust, and authority. Because humans are social beings, such problems can have long-term negative consequences for survivors' well-being.

❑ Disturbed Relatedness

Jennifer

Jennifer is a 32-year-old woman, employed as a psychiatric nurse, who has recently joined a self-help group, Women Who Love Too Much. Sexually, physically, and psychologically abused by both parents for most of her childhood and adolescence, she is also a member of an Incest Survivors Anonymous (ISA) group. Jennifer is sometimes difficult for people to understand; at times she seems sad, clinging, almost ingratiating in a childish, passive sort of way, and yet at other times she is verbally sharp, sarcastic, and overtly distrustful.

In her Women Who Love Too Much group, Jennifer describes her fear of intimacy, and her ambivalence: "I need men, I always have to have one. But I'm afraid of anyone who gets too close. I'm like a yo-yo: back and forth. First, I want them close to take care of me, but then I push them away. I think they're wonderful, and then they turn out to be [expletive]." Although Jennifer refuses to acknowledge this in either group, the men she seeks out are frequently violent toward her, and often fail to respect her in important ways. Last night, in her ISA group, she tentatively speculated that her attraction to "macho" men may be because she knows that they are incapable of "getting too close."

Interpersonal sequelae of child abuse may be understood as arising from two sources: immediate cognitive and conditioned responses to victimization that extend into the long term (e.g., distrust of others, anger and/or fear of those with greater power, concerns about abandonment, perceptions of injustice, low self-esteem) and accommodation responses to ongoing maltreatment (e.g., avoidance, passivity, sexualization, adversariality, and ingratiation) or abuse-related distress. These various reactions and responses, although understandable given the survivor's early life history, nevertheless interfere with daily interpersonal functioning and, thus, access to critical social resources such as relationships, acceptance, and support.

INTIMACY DISTURBANCE

As noted above, most child abuse occurs in the context of relationships or intimacy. As a result, it is not uncommon for abused children to fear, distrust, or experience ambivalence about interpersonal closeness. Sexual abuse survivors, for example, often report difficulties in forming and sustaining intimate relationships (Courtois, 1988; Elliott & Gabrielson-Cabush, 1990; Finkelhor et al., 1989), as do many adults with histories of other forms of childhood maltreatment (McCann & Pearlman, 1990).

The intimacy problems of abuse survivors appear to center primarily on ambivalence and fear regarding interpersonal attachment and vulnerability. Although sexual abuse is most frequently associated with later intimacy dysfunction, ambivalence about close human connections may develop even prior to the onset of such maltreatment, as has been documented in infants who were physically abused or neglected, or who had psychologically unavailable parents (Egeland et al., 1983; Main & Weston, 1981).

The insecure or ambivalent attachment that Egeland et al.'s (1983) children formed in the first months of life appears to manifest at age 5 or 6 as social withdrawal and problems in relating to other children (Ericksen et al., in press), and probably lasts into adolescence and adulthood. Although we may only speculate about the interpersonal behavior of the children in this study as they grow to maturity, it seems likely that they will be fearful and avoidant of close human connections and yet, perhaps, also fear abandonment and aloneness. It may be that many of the "loner," socially phobic, or schizoid adults presenting to psychotherapists today were quite similar to

Egeland et al.'s insecurely attached subjects as children. Certainly, it is the experience of many therapists that clients with histories of parental neglect or emotional unavailability are prone to chronic fears of abandonment, alienation, and perceived isolation in personal relationships, and yet may simultaneously exhibit anxiety in the face of increasing interpersonal closeness.

Perhaps one of the most disruptive and painful aspects of child abuse is its impact on the survivor's ability to trust. Requiring as it does a suspension of defensive activities and an assumption of safety at the hands of another, trust is especially difficult for most people who were severely maltreated as children—at least in the absence of supportive long-term relationships or extensive psychotherapy. Just as most soldiers would find it foolhardy to expose themselves willingly to the enemy during battle, so survivors often find it exceedingly hard to trust important individuals in their lives, regardless of those persons' status as friends, lovers, or colleagues.

The untreated survivor's expectation of continued victimization, difficulties with trust, adversarial perspective, and tendency to "overreact" to perceived rejection or devaluation may lead to considerable isolation from—and rejection by—the social milieu. As a result, true friendships may be rare for such survivors, as may be enduring romantic relationships. Similarly, the survivor may have considerable difficulty bonding with a psychotherapist; instead, he or she may see the clinician either as a potential enemy or as someone who must be groomed, bribed, or manipulated into providing interpersonal safety. One of the most powerful impacts of successful abuse-focused psychotherapy is, in fact, the chronic and reliable debunking of the notion of inevitable danger in close human relationships.

ALTERED SEXUALITY

Clinical experience suggests that adolescents and adults who were sexually abused as children are particularly likely to report difficulties in the sexual domain (Maltz, 1988). Such problems may present as (a) sexual dysfunction, related to fears of vulnerability and revictimization, as noted earlier; (b) a general distrust of sex partners and of men or women in general (Courtois, 1979; Jehu et al., 1984-1985; Meiselman, 1978); (c) a tendency, despite such fear and distrust, to be dependent upon or to overidealize those with whom the survivor forms romantic relationships (Courtois, 1988; Elliott & Gabrielson-Cabush, 1990; Herman, 1981); (d) preoccupation with sexual thoughts and a propensity to sexualize what otherwise might be nonsexual relationships (Courtois, 1988); and (e) a history of multiple, superficial, often quite brief sexual relationships that quickly end as intimacy develops (Courtois, 1979; Herman, 1981).

Empirical support for the notion that sexual abuse especially confers sexual problems has been provided by data indicating that sexually abused children and young adolescents are more likely than their peers to display age-inappropriate sexual awareness and behavior (for reviews, see Friedrich, 1990, 1991). Research conducted by Briere and colleagues similarly suggests that, when compared with physical and psychological abuse, sexual molestation is especially associated with high rates of dysfunctional sexual behavior in adulthood (see, e.g., Briere et al., 1992; Briere & Runtz, 1990b).

In a related area, a recent study supports the common clinical impression that sexual abuse survivors seem especially prone to sexual fantasy. Smiljanich, Briere, and Henschel (1990) found that adults molested as children reported more sexual fantasies of consensual sex, forcing others into sex, being forced into sex, involvement in an orgy, and sex with strangers than did their nonabused cohorts. Further, women with molestation histories reported more sexual fantasies of being forced into intercourse than did women without such histories or men regardless of abuse status. The researchers hypothesize that the traumatic sexualization associated with childhood sexual abuse increases molestation survivors' preoccupation with sexual thoughts, and that the coexistence of sexual and aggressive stimuli during abuse might produce a conditioned association between the two that emerges during fantasy.

The sexualized behavior and sexual preoccupation found in some adults molested as children appear to be, at first glance, antithetical to their childhood experiences of betrayal in the context of sexual interactions. One might expect that an individual who was sexually exploited while dependent upon a powerful other would be especially avoidant of sexual thoughts or behavior later in life. It is likely, however, that both avoidance and sexualization are present in many adults molested as children. On one hand, the survivor has directly experienced, and therefore fears, the potential for sexual interactions to involve exploitation, betrayal, and trauma. He or she may similarly avoid sexual thoughts because of their fear-inducing or painful associations. On the other hand, the survivor learned at an early age that one of the only ways of gaining desperately needed interpersonal closeness and nurturance was sexuality and sexual availability. Additionally, the survivor's premature introduction to sexual matters and (in some cases) sexual feelings, enhanced by their importance to the perpetrator and others, may easily lead to increased interest in and preoccupation with sex. As a result, some adolescents and adults molested as children report periods of extensive sexual behavior, often with a number of different partners (Courtois, 1979; Herman, 1981; Meiselman, 1978). The frequent yet short-lived nature of these sexual encounters can thus be understood in terms of the survivor's need for nurturance and love, which she or he has learned can best be gained through sex, and yet, simultaneously, the survivor's historically valid fears of injury, exploitation, and/or abandonment in similar intimate situations.

ASSUMPTIONS REGARDING AGGRESSION IN RELATIONSHIPS

Based upon childhood experiences of victimization by one or more caretakers, significant numbers of adult abuse survivors appear to associate relationships with maltreatment. As a result, they may either (a) avoid interpersonal closeness altogether or (b) accept some level of aggression in intimate relationships as normal or appropriate. Women in the latter group may be prone to sexual or physical victimization by others, perhaps especially in sexual/romantic relationships (McCord, 1985; Runtz, 1987; Russell, 1986). The seeming passivity, dependence, or helplessness displayed by such women may be labeled erroneously as "masochistic" by those who underestimate the extent to which women and children are socialized to be subordinate to men in our culture (Burt, 1980; Straus, Gelles, & Steinmetz, 1980) and the child abuse victim's specific training by her perpetrator to accept violence as a given in intimate relationships (Runtz & Briere, 1988), as well as the impact of impaired self-reference as described earlier.

Male abuse survivors' expectation of abuse or violence in relationships, on the other hand, may translate into a greater willingness to victimize or aggress against their partners, spouses, peers, or children, as has been shown in a number of studies (e.g., Briere & Runtz, 1989b; Pollock et al., 1990; Smiljanich, 1992; Stukas-Davis, 1990; Zaidi, Knutson, & Mehm, 1989). On a clinical level, it appears that such males may use aggression as a way to accomplish interpersonal goals (e.g., to engender respect, establish dominance, or enforce servitude), as well as to discourage historically dangerous intimacy and maintain interpersonal distance. This conversion of childhood victimization into adult perpetration is thought to arise from (a) the likelihood that the abuser's childhood perpetrator was also male, and thus may have served as a role model for aggressive behavior in relationships, as well as (b) the susceptibility of such individuals to social messages supporting the use of violence, or at least dominance, by males in relationships with less powerful others. Modern texts on the treatment of wife batterers, for example, directly consider the role of childhood victimization in men's aggressive behavior in intimate relationships, as well as their sex role training to use violence to establish interpersonal control (Sonkin, Martin, & Walker, 1985; Stordeur & Stille, 1989).

ADVERSARIALITY AND "MANIPULATION"

Although rarely identified as such in the empirical literature, the tendency for abuse survivors to view the world as a battleground—where one endeavors to win (or lose) in order to survive—is well known to abuse-specializing clinicians. By virtue of childhood experience, former abuse victims tend to assume that the world is a hostile environment, where nothing is inherently deserved and thus nothing is ever freely given. From this perspective, the survivor may conclude that the only way to gain needed things or resources is to trade other things for them, or to trick someone into providing them. Initially a way of accommodating to or coping with severe abuse, the adversariality of the growing abuse victim is often reinforced by what remains, in many ways, an abusive environment in his or her later years.

A version of the adversarial perspective may be especially present in those who were sexually abused as children. For many survivors, the basic transaction has always centered on sex: As children, they learned that their sexual parts and sexual availability were their most precious qualities to powerful others, and that such beings would do or risk many things to have sexual contact with them. Perhaps the most obvious example of the sexual adversariality assumed by some sexual abuse survivors is that of prostitution. As Sandra Butler (1979) notes:

> Even before puberty a girl often learns to use her sexuality to please her father. After several years she may see prostitution as a logical extension of selling sex at home. Many abused women decide that if they have to have sex with a man, they might as well get paid for it. (p. 41)

Probably as a result of this dynamic, several recent studies demonstrate a link between childhood sexual abuse and later involvement in prostitution in adolescence or adulthood (Bagley & Young, 1987; Silbert & Pines, 1981). For those not involved in prostitution, however, survivors' experience of the value others place on their sexual aspects can still lead to the assumption that sex is the best way to initiate or sustain an intimate relationship, receive (superficially) caring attention, or gain interpersonal power (Butler, 1979; Herman, 1981). Unfortunately, the survivor's sexual value is often relatively transient for many of those to whom she wishes to relate, resulting in eventual experiences of abandonment or rejection.

Abuse-related adversariality is not, of course, restricted to the sexual domain, nor is such a perspective limited to sexual abuse survivors. Child abuse may teach the victim about not only his or her ultimate sexual value to others, but also the value of being good, acquiescent, passive, selfless, and so on in interactions with powerful others. For example, the child who discovers that servile attention to his or her abuser's various needs can forestall impending violence or elicit rare praise or affection is likely to conclude that powerful ones should be groomed and catered to, in exchange for love or forestalled abandonment. This perspective may, in part, further explain the behavior of the "passive" battered woman described earlier, who may tolerate violent or abusive behavior from her spouse or partner in order to retain a sense of being loved or feeling needed.

Although many therapists can understand the abuse survivor's trading of sex or acquiescence for love, security, or acceptance, fewer are as supportive when the other side of the adversariality dynamic occurs: that of "manipulation." As generally understood, this term refers to those superficially nonaggressive behaviors engaged in by an individual in order to extract goods and/or services from those who would not bestow them otherwise. From the survivor's perspective, however, manipulation is a historically appropriate survival behavior, based on (a) powerful needs for certain interpersonal supplies; (b) the assumption that nothing in this world is freely given and that, at any rate, the survivor does not inherently deserve gifts; and (c) his or her previously developed skills at extracting needed resources from a hostile environment (Briere, 1989).

Of the many ways in which a desperate, often angry person can psychologically coerce those around her or him to bestow needed interpersonal supplies, perhaps the two most problematic for family members, lovers, and therapists are suicidal "gestures" and interpersonally motivated self-mutilation. The former, often referred to as *parasuicidality*, occurs when the individual engages in potentially life-threatening behavior (e.g., wrist slashing, drug overdoses) as a way to force personally important individuals to express caring, attention, validation, or appreciation. Interpersonally motivated self-mutilation, on the other hand, does not occur in the context of threatened death, but rather as a dramatic method of controlling the responses of important others in one's life in order to receive greater attention or nurturance from them (Ross & McKay, 1979; Walsh & Rosen, 1988).[1]

Thus, for example, the self-mutilating survivor who carves on his wrists with razors or who burns herself with cigarette embers just prior to a psychotherapy session may be seeking to communicate to the therapist that (a) therapy hurts, (b) therapy is inadequate to deal with the pain, or (c) "You better stop being hurtful and be more loving, or I will continue to visibly injure myself and make you feel like a bad clinician."

Despite the theoretical appropriateness of manipulative behavior in light of the survivor's childhood experience, the net result of tricking or coercing others is usually estrangement from them. Thus the survivor may become caught in a vicious cycle: (a) Neediness and perceived undeservingness motivate manipulativeness toward others, who, (b) although perhaps briefly awarding the desired behavior or object, eventually respond with anger and rejection or abandonment, producing (c) greater dysphoria and emptiness in the survivor, and further (often more desperate) manipulation.

AGGRESSION

The last form of disturbed relatedness considered here is that of aggressive behavior. Empirical studies and clinical experience both suggest that children's aggressiveness toward others—commonly expressed as fighting, bullying, or attacking other children—is a frequent short-term sequel of various types of maltreatment: physical abuse (e.g., George & Main, 1979; Reidy, 1977), sexual molestation (e.g., Erickson et al., 1989; Gomes-Schwartz et al., 1990), psychological abuse and emotional unavailability (e.g., Egeland, 1989; Vissing et al., 1991), and having been raised by one or more alcoholic parents (e.g., Chafetz, Blane, & Hill, 1971). In general, it appears that such behavior represents a generic externalization of the child's abuse-related trauma and dysphoria, as well as, perhaps, the effects of modeling the abusive parent's behavior. As noted by several writers, the net effect of this angry aggression is often social isolation and unpopularity (e.g., Egeland, 1989), milieu responses to the aggressive child that may increase the likelihood of his or her further violence toward others.

Interestingly, the literature on the long-term impacts of child abuse on aggressive behavior appears to implicate sexual abuse histories specifically in sexually aggressive behavior and physical abuse in physically aggressive behavior. Certain adolescent and adult sexual abuse survivors, in this regard, appear to be more prone to victimize children or women sexually (e.g., Langevin, Handy, Hook, Day, & Russon, 1985; Rokous, Carter, & Prentky, 1988; Stukas-Davis, 1990), whereas the majority of studies of child abuse and adult aggression have found links to childhood histories of physical maltreatment (e.g., McCord, 1983; Pollock et al., 1990; Widom, 1989). Data supportive of the specificity of physical child abuse in the etiology of adult physical aggression have recently been offered by Briere and Runtz (1990b), who found that subjects' scores on an aggression scale were uniquely related to childhood histories of physical (as opposed to psychological or sexual) abuse.

The potential role of physical abuse in the development of adult violent tendencies suggests that resolution of repetitive aggressive criminality in adults may not be best served by punishment (e.g., incarceration) alone, but rather by abuse-specific treatment in the context of a controlled environment. There are very few data available, however, on the efficacy of abuse-focused psychotherapy in the recidivism of violent offenders, despite the potential social and humanitarian value of such an endeavor were it to be successful. Future research on the locked/residential abuse-focused treatment of violent perpetrators is highly indicated in this area, and may yield fruit for both the aggressive individual and society at large.

❑   **Avoidance**

Richard

Richard has attended a 12-step program for drug addicts for more than four years, and has just recently joined a similar group for "sex addicts." Despite the support of these groups, he often finds himself returning to a variety of self-destructive activities as a way to "blank out my past and forget my life." When involved in drinking or drug binges, Richard has been known to use combinations of various potent drugs (including heroin, cocaine, PCP, and amphetamines), sometimes while drinking up to a liter of hard liquor a day. When able to control his substance abuse, he often engages in compulsive, seemingly indiscriminate sexual contact with men he picks up in bars. Although his last HIV test was negative, he notes without obvious concern that "it's just a matter of time."

Richard was repeatedly assaulted and victimized by his father and paternal uncle as a child and adolescent. These acts of abuse were especially cruel and often bizarre, including being tied to a tractor overnight, urinated upon, shot with a pellet gun, and forced to drink large quantities of whiskey until he became sick. Although he was twice treated for broken bones as an adolescent, he never disclosed the true reasons for his injuries to doctors or nurses, for fear of retaliation from his father.

Many abuse survivors report utilizing behavioral strategies to avoid or attenuate dysphoria related to childhood abuse experiences. Because these coping responses often occur on an unconscious level, and sometimes work quite well, they may not be recognized as abuse related by either the survivor or his or her therapist. For example, the individual whose compulsive use of alcohol or drugs effectively keeps abuse memories out of awareness, or whose cognitive defenses completely eliminate knowledge of sexual victimization, is likely to view her or his "addictions" or memory blanks as individual problems unrelated to childhood trauma.

Among the "dysfunctional" activities associated with avoidance of abuse-specific memories and affects are psychoactive substance use, self-mutilation, compulsive sexual activity, bulimia, and, in the extreme case, suicidality. In each instance, the problem behavior may represent a conscious or unconscious choice to (as one survivor put it) "go with the lesser of two evils"—involvement in seemingly dysfunctional and/or self-destructive behaviors rather than experiencing the considerable pain of complete abuse-specific awareness.

USE OF PSYCHOACTIVE SUBSTANCES

Often even more powerful than dissociative states, alcohol and psychoactive drugs are immediate "painkillers" for many individuals who suffer from anxiety, depression, or upsetting memories. The acute effects of alcohol and drugs are manifold:

- temporary attenuation or elimination of dysphoria
- inducement of some level of euphoria or relative well-being
- interference with memory of painful events
- for some individuals, provision of an opportunity to express painful affect (e.g., sadness, rage) that might otherwise be inhibited

- provision of an opportunity for the user to develop a minimally demanding peer or support group (i.e., other users)

The power of such chemicals can be seen in recent statistics regarding the incidence of alcoholism and other drug addiction in our culture: Literally millions of North Americans require nonprescription psychoactive substances on a daily basis, such that they are considered drug addicts, alcoholics, or both. Given what we know about the long-term sequelae of child abuse, it is not surprising that adults abused as children especially seek the chemically induced dissociation bestowed by alcohol and other drugs.

Perhaps the best-known link between childhood maltreatment and adolescent or adult substance abuse involves the tendency for children of alcoholics to be addicts or alcoholics themselves later in life. Winoker, Cadoret, Dorzab, and Baker (1971), for example, found that adult children of alcoholics have about a 15% chance of also becoming alcoholic. Similarly, Claydon's (1987) study of 1,302 college freshmen indicated that parental alcoholism was related to students' later use of both alcohol and drugs.

Part of the association between parental and offspring substance abuse, at least in terms of the intergenerational transmission of alcoholism, may involve genetic or biological factors. The various studies in this area provide persuasive data that there may be a physiological vulnerability to alcoholism that is at least partially inherited by first-degree relatives (e.g., D. W. Goodwin, 1979; Pollock, Schneider, Gabrielli, & Goodwin, 1987; Shukitt, Goodwin, & Winoker, 1972).

More relevant to the current discussion, however, are the conclusions of researchers such as Cloninger (1983) and Donald Goodwin (1984) that the alcoholism of many individuals cannot be explained by genetic influences alone, and probably arises primarily from psychological factors present in their families of origin. It is likely that the most important of these psychological/familial factors are the psychological (and sometimes physical and/or sexual) abuse and neglect of soon-to-be-alcoholic children by their alcoholic parents (Elliott & Edwards, 1991) and the modeling such parents provide regarding the use of psychologically anesthetic substances during times of stress.

The relationship between other forms of child maltreatment and substance abuse is equally clear. Sexual abuse, for example, has been linked to later substance abuse or addiction (including alcoholism) in a variety of studies (e.g., Briere & Woo, 1991; Dembo et al., 1989; Rohsenow, Corbett, & Devine, 1988), as has physical child abuse (e.g., Dembo et al., 1989; Gil, 1988). Illustrative of the strength of this potential association are the findings of Briere and Runtz (1987) that sexually abused female crisis center clients had 10 times the likelihood of a drug addiction history and more than twice the likelihood of an alcoholism history than a comparison group of female crisis clients who had not been sexually abused as children.

Despite the assumptions of a society that has recently "declared war on drugs" and that entreats adolescents to "just say no" to such substances, the current data suggest that the maladaptive use of alcohol and drugs cannot be so simplistically addressed. Instead, these findings indicate that substance abuse is often inextricably associated with chronic childhood experiences of maltreatment and pain, and that such substances are often used for temporary relief of—and survival despite—postabuse trauma.

SUICIDALITY

The ultimate avoidance strategy may be suicide. As noted by Schneidman (1985), escape from extreme psychic pain (i.e., severe depression, crippling anxiety, overwhelmingly painful memories, or extreme hopelessness) is a commonly expressed motivation for suicide. In contrast to suicidal activities that are engaged in for interpersonal goals (e.g., attention, support, validation, as noted earlier in this chapter), actual death-seeking behavior can represent a search for complete surcease. As many survivors have put it, "I just want everything to stop," or "I want to stop hurting forever." Many such suicidal individuals do not actually desire death per se, but rather seek an end to a pain-ridden life. Because other, less final, coping strategies have repeatedly failed to provide enduring symptom relief, the escape-motivated suicidal person's experience of hopelessness leads him or her to, in the words of one sexual abuse survivor, "the last out."

Almost all of the research literature on the relationship between childhood maltreatment and later suicidal behavior has been limited to sexual abuse, although it is clear from a clinical viewpoint that chronic childhood psychological abuse can also be a significant contributor to later suicidality. Most studies of adolescents or adults who were molested as children document more frequent suicidal behavior and/or greater suicidal ideation among survivors relative to their nonabused peers (e.g., Bagley & Ramsay, 1986; Scalzo, 1991).

In studies of abuse-related suicidality conducted by Briere and colleagues, the likelihood of at least one suicide attempt in the past has ranged from 51% to 79% in three samples of sexually abused female crisis intervention clients (Briere & Runtz, 1986, 1987; Briere, Evans, Runtz, & Wall, 1988), one sample of sexually abused male crisis intervention clients (Briere et al., 1988), and two samples of sexually abused female psychiatric emergency room patients (Briere & Woo, 1991; Briere & Zaidi, 1989). In contrast, the average suicide attempt rate for nonabused comparison groups in these studies was 30%.

The link between child abuse history and later suicidal behavior epitomizes the potential risks to victims and society that accrue from child maltreatment. This connection is all the more significant given that the suicidality statistics reported above are for *unsuccessful* attempts, that is, from those individuals who lived to make such reports. The extent of completed suicides among child abuse v: ·· remains unknown.

TENSION-REDUCING BEHAVIORS

Much has been written about the "acting out," "poor impulse control," and "addictions" of those who, in retrospect, have histories of childhood victimization. The first description suggests that abuse survivors tend to externalize their conflicts and issues, and writers who address "acting out" often stress the angry or dramatic components of such behaviors. An "impulse control" perspective, on the other hand, implies that the survivor suffers from a specific inability to inhibit behavioral responses to needs, frustration, or affect—drive states that others successfully control. Regardless of framework, both of these conceptualizations tend to agree on the behaviors most problematic in this area: indiscriminate and frequent sexual activity, substance abuse, binging or chronic overeating, spending sprees, risk-taking activities, and self-mutilation.

Others have explained similar activities in terms of addictive processes. It is not unusual, for example, to hear therapists or self-help group members speak of sex addicts, food addicts, exercise addicts, work addicts, relationship addicts, thrill addicts, or, more generally, of addictive personalities when describing the repetitively excessive behavior of some individuals.[2] By utilizing a term previously reserved for biological dependence on drugs or alcohol, this perspective emphasizes the pull such behaviors have for chronic repetition in susceptible individuals, and the resultant interference with daily functioning that can ensue. As noted by Peele and Brodsky (1991), however, there are a number of other assumptions that underlie the concept of addiction, regardless of whether it involves dependence on a biological substance. These include that addiction is a form of disease and thus is genetically inherited or biologically determined; that addictive behavior represents a complete loss of personal control and thus reflects powerlessness; that addiction "inevitably expands until it takes over and destroys your life" (p. 24); and that addiction "requires medical and/or spiritual treatment" (p. 25).

The perspective offered in this book is that the various behaviors described above relate less to acting out, impulse control problems, or addictions than they do to the overwhelming dysphoric tension experienced by many abuse survivors. In the face of extreme abuse-related distress, often restimulated by revictimization and/or perceived abandonment or rejection, the survivor may engage in any of a number of external activities that anesthetize, soothe, interrupt, or forestall painful affect.

This tension-reduction response pattern is thought to be learned during and following severe child abuse experiences, when any form of pain avoidance is likely to be reinforced. Over time, the survivor learns to deal with acute or impending abuse-related distress by quickly resorting to distracting, calming, or anesthetizing behaviors, along with the dissociative responses outlined earlier. Because overwhelming abuse-related emotional pain typically began before the young victim had developed more sophisticated ways of dealing with distress, however, such activities are typically quite primitive. Further, the immediate effectiveness of dissociative and tension-reducing responses lessens the need to learn more sophisticated methods of affect tolerance and modulation (what are referred to in this book as *affect regulation skills*), a trade-off that, unfortunately, leaves the survivor with few internal coping responses to pain or distress. As a result, a vicious cycle ensues: Early abuse-related tension-reduction behaviors and dissociation inhibit the development of more sophisticated affect regulation skills, which, in turn, leaves the survivor with few options but additional dissociation and tension-reduction behaviors in the face of further psychological pain.

Clinical experience suggests that abuse-related tension-reducing behaviors often occur in a relatively predictable series of steps:

1. The survivor experiences or anticipates an interpersonal stressor, usually involving perceived abandonment, unfairness, betrayal, or significant conflict with a love or authority figure.
2. This stressor, because of its similarity to unresolved childhood abuse issues, restimulates or exacerbates powerful feelings of rage, anxiety, helplessness, self-loathing, and/or emptiness.
3. The seemingly unbearable psychic pressure arising from these internal states, in combination with the survivor's abuse-related dread of painful feelings and relative lack of affect regulation skills, motivates (a) a tendency toward dissociation, including detachment from anxiety or guilt about the consequences of potentially self-injurious acts and (b) a search for any means of tension reduction.
4. The survivor responds with activities designed to provide one or more of the following:
   temporary distraction
   interruption of dissociative or dysphoric states
   anesthesia of psychic pain
   restoration of control
   distress-incompatible sensory input
   temporary filling of perceived emptiness
   self-soothing
   specific relief from guilt or self-hatred
   Because these behaviors are responses to affects or memories that have been to some extent dissociated, the survivor may experience her or his responses as impulsively chosen or ego-dystonic—as though they had emerged "from out of nowhere."

5. Due to the effectiveness of these distress-reducing behaviors, a sense of calm and palpable relief ensues, at least for some period of time. Also present, however, may be subsequent guilt or self-disgust at having engaged in such activities, as well as a growing sense of not being in control of one's actions—feelings that may motivate the need for further avoidance behavior in the near future.

6. Ultimately, the use of tension-reducing mechanisms in the future is reinforced, based on what is essentially an avoidance learning paradigm: Behavior that reduces pain is likely to be repeated in the presence or threat of further pain.

From this perspective, a considerable proportion of the "addictive" or "compulsive" behavior of abuse survivors may pertain less to difficulties in inhibiting impulses per se, or to the uncontrollable effects of a powerful disease process, than to the seemingly intolerable dysphoria anticipated or experienced by such individuals in certain interpersonal situations. Such dysphoria may motivate repetitive involvement in activities that are ultimately self-injurious, but that have the immediate impact of reducing or forestalling psychic stress or pain.

It is important to reiterate that this tension-reduction perspective emphasizes not only the survivor's difficulties in internally modulating or accommodating to painful affect, but also the extent of distress (based upon both historic and contemporary events) that he or she experiences. For example, the sexual abuse survivor who is rejected by a lover and "acts out" as a result is likely to be responding to a dysphoria overload: not only the experience of rejection and loss that most people would feel at the undesired end of a relationship, but also the restimulation of long-standing childhood injury involving themes of betrayal and abandonment in intimate contexts. Without an understanding of this combined trauma, the outside observer might easily view the survivor's behavior as an "overreaction" to a relatively minor stressor, and as reflective of an inherent inability to tolerate painful affect per se.

As indicated by McCann and Pearlman (1990), the absolute extent of distress the survivor experiences is partially determined by the survivor's capacity to self-soothe and otherwise handle or tolerate painful affect, the support he or she receives from the social environment, and the cognitive schema (e.g., beliefs, assumptions, expectations) he or she invokes to understand the pain. Thus we may understand the often extreme desperation experienced by the child abuse survivor, who not only must deal with a combination of early and contemporary injury, but who additionally lacks the affective skills and external resources necessary to cope adaptively with such trauma. In such a context, self-mutilation or sexual activity may appear to represent the survivor's best option for moderating or dampening aversive internal experience.

Although many repetitively invoked behaviors may serve as tension-reduction devices (including, perhaps, behaviors normally associated with the compulsive aspects of obsessive-compulsive disorder), three are especially noteworthy for their frequent presentation in adolescent and adult abuse survivors: self-mutilation, compulsive sexual behavior, and binging and purging.

Self-Mutilation

Defined by Walsh and Rosen (1988) as "deliberate, non-life-threatening, self-effected bodily harm or disfigurement of a socially unacceptable nature" (p. 10), self-mutilation most typically involves repetitious cutting or carving of the body or limbs, burning of the skin with cigarettes, or hitting of the head or body against or with objects. Other types of deliberate self-injury also occur, however, including irritation or wounding of the eyes; excoriation of the skin; self-inflicted injury to the nose, mouth, or tongue; and genital mutilation.

Most of these forms of self-injury have been shown to occur among survivors of severe child abuse. Self-mutilation in adolescents and adults has been associated with childhood histories of sexual abuse (Briere, Henschel, Smiljanich, & Morlan-Magallanes, 1990; van der Kolk, Perry, & Herman, 1991; Walsh & Rosen, 1988) as well as other types of childhood maltreatment (Briere et al., 1990; Walsh & Rosen, 1988).

Various researchers have hypothesized that self-mutilating behavior serves temporarily to reduce the psychic tension associated with extremely negative affect, self-loathing and guilt, intense depersonalization, feelings of helplessness, and/or painfully fragmented thought processes (e.g., Grunebaum & Klerman, 1967; Gardner & Gardner, 1975; Jones, Congin, Stevenson, Straus, & Frei, 1979), psychological states all too common for survivors of severe abuse. Although often immediately effective, such behavior is rarely adaptive in the long term, leading to repeated cycles of self-injury, subsequent calm, and the slow building of further tension. As noted by Walsh and Rosen (1988):

> The intent of self-mutilating acts is generally to alleviate distress in the short term. . . . For chronic repeaters, the self-mutilating acts are clearly not permanent solutions. Their behavior becomes an accepted method to modulate and reduce internal tension. It is a method to which they can return again and again and employ on an as-needed basis. (p. 44)

The fact that self-mutilation can serve functions as disparate as distraction from psychic pain and self-inflicted punishment may explain the tendency for such behaviors to continue over long periods of time and to resist standard treatment approaches (Walsh & Rosen, 1988).

Compulsive Sexual Behavior

Also found among some abuse survivors are periods of frequent, short-term sexual behaviors, most typically with a number of different sexual partners.[3] As noted earlier, the choice of multiple sexual partners by some sexual abuse survivors appears to represent powerful needs for closeness and intimacy, as a result of deprivation in these areas in the past, and, yet, fearfulness regarding the vulnerability inherent in sustained intimacy. More relevant to the notion of tension reduction, however, is a second motive for frequent and/or rapidly initiated sexual behavior: the use of sex for distraction, excitement, and avoidance of emptiness. As described earlier, sexual activity can have the temporary ability to soothe, mask, or dispel chronic abuse-related dysphoria. For example, many abuse survivors report involvement in frequent "one-night stands" or repetitive masturbation during times of depression, loneliness, or perceived abandonment or rejection by others, or during periods of uncontrollable rumination and recall of abuse-related painful events. For such individuals, "inappropriate" or "excessive" sexual activity is, instead, a consciously or unconsciously chosen coping mechanism invoked to modulate painful internal experience.

Binging and Purging

Clinicians working in the area of eating disorders have noted recently that individuals with such problems seem especially likely to report child abuse histories. Various aspects of disturbed eating behavior have been empirically or anecdotally associated with sexual abuse (Kearney-Cooke, 1988; Steiger & Zanko, 1990; Root & Fallon, 1988), physical abuse (Root & Fallon, 1988), and parental alcoholism (Claydon, 1987). Interestingly, other studies have either failed to find a relationship between child abuse and later eating disturbance (e.g., Finn, Hartman, Leon, & Lawson, 1986) or found that only certain forms of eating disorder are associated with child maltreatment. With respect to the latter, it appears that childhood sexual abuse may be associated specifically with bulimic binging and purging, whereas (nonbinging) anorexia nervosa may be either uncorrelated or negatively related to sexual molestation history (Piran, Lerner, Garfinkel, Kennedy, & Brouillete, 1988; Steiger & Zanko, 1990).

The specific association between sexual molestation and bulimia, but not anorexia, is supported by research suggesting that parents of bulimics are often more dysfunctional, intrusive, and aggressive (Strober & Humphrey, 1987), and thus potentially more abusive (Steiger & Zanko, 1990). Parents of anorexics, on the other hand, are frequently characterized as overcontrolled and distant (e.g., Bruch, 1973), and thus more likely to be emotionally neglectful than sexually or physically abusive. Additionally, bulimia is often described as a cyclic response to interpersonal stressors and painful affect (Muuss, 1986), much as has been demonstrated for abuse-related self-mutilation.

Root and Fallon (1989) suggest that binge-purge behaviors can operate as "both a reaction to and a method of coping with physical and sexual abuse" (p. 90). In general agreement with the perspective offered in this book, these authors list nine functions of bulimia, including "a way to 'anesthetize' intense 'negative' feelings associated with the victimization experience such as rage, pain, fear, and powerlessness" (p. 93) and "a way to cope with stress and relieve tension" (p. 95).

Sexual abuse survivors who display bulimic behavior frequently describe escalating dysphoria, self-denigrating cognitions, intrusive thoughts and memories regarding childhood abuse experiences, and a painful sense of emptiness—all of which respond to the soothing, distracting, and filling effects of rapid and extensive self-feeding. Unfortunately, subsequent to the survivor's binge there is often intense guilt and self-disgust, motivating, in turn, purging of the ingested food via vomiting, laxatives, or extensive exercise.

❏ Abuse Effects as "Codependence"

As noted frequently in this book, adults with histories of child hood maltreatment often encounter problems in their relations with others. Among other difficulties, there may be involvement in destructive relationships, wherein the survivor is often revictimized. There may be hunger for intimacy and yet fears of injury, rejection, or abandonment. There is often dependency and need for approval in the same interpersonal context where the survivor feels rageful and overwhelmed by obsessive concerns about control. I have suggested that such powerful, contradictory affects and needs arise from the fact that child abuse occurs in the most primary of relationships—in contexts where support and nurturance should be foremost, but where, instead, pain and betrayal exist.

Recently, however, another perspective has been offered regarding the kinds of behaviors described above—that of "codependency" (e.g., Beattie, 1987; Bradshaw, 1988; Schaef, 1986). Perhaps not surprisingly, many of those who identify themselves as codependent (or who are labeled as such by others) also report childhood histories of sexual abuse, maltreatment by an alcoholic parent, or other forms of victimization. In the same vein, members of self-help groups whose focus is codependency frequently spend considerable time discussing their "dysfunctional families" of origin, wherein sexual or physical abuse often took place.

The term *codependency* has undergone substantial revision since its introduction in the early 1980s by Alcoholics Anonymous, Al-Anon, and (soon thereafter) family therapists. Initially defined as, for example, "ill health, or maladaptive or problematic behavior that is associated with living, working with, or otherwise being close to a person with alcoholism" (Whitfield, 1984, cited in Schaef, 1986, p. 17), the original intent was to describe the behavior of someone somehow connected to a substance-dependent individual whose behavior not only supported ("enabled") the individual's addiction, but also reflected a functional reliance on the individual's problem with alcohol or drugs. For example, the wife of an alcoholic might be confronted in her codependency group regarding ways in which she subtly encouraged her husband's drinking, and, furthermore, used his alcoholic behavior to meet her own needs to be needed, or to avoid interactions with the social milieu.

More recently, however, the concept of codependency has been broadened to include relationships with almost anyone who has a chronic psychological or behavioral problem, and has extended the diagnosis of addiction onto those so related. For example, Beattie (1987) states that "a codependent person is one who has let another person's behavior affect him or her, and who is obsessed with controlling that person's behavior" (p. 31), whereas Schaef (1986) states:

> Co-dependents are relationship addicts who frequently use a relationship in the same way drunks use alcohol: to get a "fix." Since co-dependents feel they have no intrinsic meaning of their own, almost all of their meaning comes from outside; they are almost completely externally referented. Persons who are so completely externally referented will do almost anything to be in a relationship, regardless of how awful the relationship is. (p. 44)

A review of the codependency literature reveals a wide variety of problems and characteristics thought to be associated with this pattern of behavior, including overinvolvement in the caretaking of others, dependence and passivity, extreme need for control (often through expressed helplessness or by guilt induction), low self-esteem, guilt, weak or permeable interpersonal boundaries, avoidance and denial of feelings, chronic depression and anxiety, hostility, extreme need for approval, and "addiction" to relationships.

The reader will note that, in many ways, descriptions of codependency and the interpersonal aspects of child abuse trauma are similar. The primary differences appear to involve the following:

1. *The mechanism whereby the behavior is thought to develop:* Codependency has to do with contact or association with a dysfunctional person (e.g., Schaef, 1986) and/or as the result of an actual disease process (see Peele & Brodsky, 1991), whereas an abuse trauma perspective specifically refers to childhood maltreatment effects.

2. *The age at which the behaviors are thought to begin:* Codependency implies that dysfunctional behavior in response to a dysfunctional person can arise at any time in the life span, whereas a child abuse trauma perspective assumes that the behavior in question was learned early in life, although its expression may be more prominent in adulthood.

3. *Theory regarding etiology:* Descriptions of codependency typically provide little concrete information about how or why codependent behavior arises (although see writers such as Peele & Brodsky, 1991; Schaef, 1986, for social theories), whereas descriptions of postabuse trauma specifically indicate that such responses are the logical extension of the survivor's childhood reactions and accommodations to victimization.

4. *Issues of responsibility:* Codependency approaches tend to stress the person's choice to be codependent (often stating, for example, that afflicted individuals have "let" other people's behavior affect them; Beattie, 1987, p. 32), whereas an abuse perspective is predicated on the notion that child abuse is never the responsibility of the victim, and that many of his or her later abuse-related responses are survival based, rather than freely chosen.

Despite these differences, many abuse survivors find value in defining themselves as codependent. Among the potential benefits are the opportunity to interact with and gain support from other survivors in a nonprofessional, self-help environment (i.e., codependency groups), as well as the reassurance to be gained by an explanatory, relatively nonstigmatizing label for some of their most distressing interpersonal problems. Finally, the codependency movement may be helpful for many abuse survivors because, in fact, it does address critical abuse-relevant relationship issues, and provides interventions (e.g., books, groups, workshops) and hope regarding the resolution of such difficulties.

In light of the material reviewed in this book, it seems likely that codependency represents one part of a larger phenomenon—that of accommodation to victimization. Codependent behavior may be understood as adaptive interpersonal strategies originally developed to survive the actions of abusive caretakers, behavior that the individual continues to use in adulthood when faced with real or perceived interpersonal danger or adversity. One can easily understand, for example, why a woman who was abused as a child might defensively present as eager to please, nonassertive, and dependent in her relationship with a controlling husband—just as she did with her original abuser—and yet also seek to control his behavior (as was also adaptive in her childhood) through the relatively less dangerous techniques of guilt induction, "passive-aggressive" behavior, and manipulation. Other characteristics attributed to codependency, such as avoidance of feelings, boundary difficulties, chronic guilt, low self-esteem, depression, anxiety, and other-directedness also are identified throughout this book as long-term impacts of childhood maltreatment.

As relevant as codependency is to childhood maltreatment, it is important that we not lose sight of the fact that such behaviors are highly congruent with the female sex role in our society. It is probable, in this regard, that the same social dynamics that support exploitation and victimization of children teach women to be passive, relationship oriented, and reluctant to express anger or personal needs directly. When such socialization pressures interact with child abuse trauma, codependent behaviors may be especially likely. Epstein and Epstein (1990) note:

> Women have been socialized to value nurturing, marriage, and family. They have traditionally been—and remain—in the position of giving to others. Ironically, being a caretaker and gaining self-respect from the responsibilities of family nurturance is part of the description of codependency. It is not surprising, then, that the population defined as being codependent is made up primarily of women. (p. 6)

Because of the overlap among the concepts of codependency, abuse trauma, and sex role expectations of femininity, the first term probably should be used carefully by clinicians working with abuse survivors. Most problematic in this regard is the tendency for co-dependency to be understood as an optional, chosen state. The chronically battered wife, for example, may be seen as a codependent who supports her husband's violence by her "continued participation" in a "dysfunctional relationship"—thereby suggesting that she is a willing coconspirator in her own victimization. In contrast, an abuse perspective would emphasize this person's socialization as a woman to be subservient to dominant men, and the likelihood that, as a child, she was further trained to accept violence and/or unhappiness as an unavoidable "given" in intimate relationships.

For many survivors of severe child abuse, life is seen as offering little in the way of self-determination or freedom. Many survivor behaviors arise from painful internal experience and victimization-based assumptions—phenomena not always understood or accepted by those with more positive life histories and more access to self-efficacy. In many cases, what others see as "dysfunctional" or "co-dependent" behavior is the survivor's search for relief from or accommodation to abuse-related helplessness, emptiness, and dysphoria, filtered through social prescriptions regarding acceptable behavior. In this context, abstract notions of free will or autonomy may be psychologically irrelevant. Similarly, analyses that simply stress responsibility and choice can easily be seen as discounting or blaming and, ultimately, a double bind in light of the survivor's perceived lack of viable options.

❑ Abuse Effects as "Borderline Personality Disorder"

Borderline personality disorder is described by DSM-III-R as a chronic personality disturbance in which there is "a pervasive pattern of instability of self-image, interpersonal relationship, and mood, beginning by early adulthood and present in a variety of contexts" (American Psychiatric Association, 1987, p. 346). DSM-III-R notes a variety of symptoms attributable to this disorder, including the following:

- "impulsiveness in at least two areas that are potentially self-damaging" (e.g., indiscriminate sex, substance abuse)
- "a pattern of unstable and intense interpersonal relationships" (e.g., idealization and devaluation)
- "inappropriate, intense anger"
- "marked and persistent identity disturbance"
- "affective instability: marked shifts from baseline mood to depression, irritability, or anxiety"
- "recurrent suicidal threats, gestures, or behavior, or self-mutilating behavior"
- "chronic feelings of emptiness and boredom"
- "frantic efforts to avoid real or imagined abandonment" (p. 347)

The reader will note that almost all of the behaviors listed have appeared in this or the previous chapter among the long-term effects of child abuse. As will be described later in this section, recent research on the life histories of "borderline" individuals do, in fact, document very high rates of childhood maltreatment. Modern theories of borderline personality disorder, however, almost without exception, do not specifically implicate child abuse in its etiology.

Writers such as Gunderson (1984), Kernberg (1976), and Masterson and Rinsley (1975) conceptualize borderline pathology as arising from developmental disruption or arrest during (at most) the first three years or so of life, such that important tasks involving separation and individuation from the principal caretaker are not accomplished. As a result, the child is thought to lack sufficient self-relatedness or self-awareness, and to form inadequately the internal representation of a good parent that otherwise would soothe and comfort the child at times of stress or separation. As Groves (1975) notes:

> Whereas in normal development the child learns to separate from important objects with sadness and anger rather than with despair and rage, the borderline cannot tolerate negative affects associated with separation and continues into adulthood the pre-Oedipal child's clinging, as if others were desperately-needed parts rather than separate persons. (p. 338)

Although many reasons have been offered for such developmental disturbance (e.g., parental abandonment, neglect, or death), most typically the mother is seen as responsible. Rinsley (1980), for example, states:

We have postulated that the mother of the future borderline child and adult, herself borderline, rewards (provides libidinal supplies and gratification to) her infant when he behaves in a dependent, clinging manner toward her, but threatens to reject or abandon . . . him when he makes efforts toward being independent of her, that is, toward separation-individuation. (p. 290)

Although frank childhood maltreatment (e.g., extreme emotional neglect, physical or sexual abuse) would seemingly operate as a powerful source of developmental disruption, this possibility has not been considered by most theoreticians in this area. As Herman and van der Kolk (1987) write:

Occasional case examples that include severe physical or sexual abuse in the background of borderline patients are found throughout the literature; generally they are reported without any comment on the possible impact of the trauma. In the main, the idea that borderline patients may in actuality have been severely abused tends to be discounted or dismissed as part of the patient's self-serving distortion of reality. (p. 114)

Despite the tendency for many psychodynamic theorists to overlook a relationship between child abuse and later borderline characteristics, a number of recent studies have demonstrated a significant link between the two. Herman, Perry, and van der Kolk (1989), for example, found that of 21 subjects diagnosed as borderline, 71% had been physically abused as children, and 67% had histories of childhood sexual abuse. These results reinforce Herman's (1986) earlier findings that 67% of 12 borderline outpatients had reported having been abused as children and Stone's (1981) data that 75% of 12 inpatients with diagnoses of borderline personality disorder had been incest victims.

More recently, Briere and Zaidi (1989) found that of 14 nonpsychotic psychiatric emergency room patients whose charts referred to borderline personality disorder or borderline traits, 93% described sexual abuse before age 17. Ogata et al. (1990) report that 71% of 24 inpatients with borderline diagnoses were sexually abused as children. A doctoral dissertation by Lobel (1990) indicates that women inpatients with a history of sexual abuse scored significantly higher on the Diagnostic Interview for Borderlines—Revised

(DIB-R; Gunderson & Zanarini, 1983) than did women with no molestation. In another dissertation, Fisher (1991) reported that 71.8% and 79.9% of 103 outpatients with (respectively) sexual or sexual and physical abuse histories scored in the clinical range (T score > 70) on the Borderline scale of the Millon Clinical Multiaxial Inventory (Millon, 1983), as opposed to only 17.1% of nonabused subjects.

Given the concordance of borderline characteristics with the known interpersonal effects of child abuse and the overrepresentation of abuse survivors among those diagnosed as borderline, it appears likely that, as with the label "codependent," the primary disturbance underlying this diagnosis involves chronic reactions and accommodations to early child abuse trauma. Although any chronic extreme form of early child abuse is probably sufficient to produce borderline symptoms in some individuals, the most powerful sequence of events contributing to borderline personality characteristics may be (a) attachment difficulties in the first few years of life, typically arising from parental abandonment, psychological abuse, or emotional neglect (as per Egeland, Sroufe, and others' research, cited in Chapter 2), followed by (b) severe and sustained childhood maltreatment in early childhood, especially sexual abuse.

Because the term *borderline personality disorder* carries with it etiologic assumptions that overlook the powerful impacts of childhood abuse and neglect and potentially misleading assumptions regarding treatment (i.e., reliance on interventions that do not address child abuse experiences as relevant, let alone critical), therapists are advised to use this diagnosis with care when working with abuse survivors.

❏ Conclusions

This chapter and the preceding one have reviewed and synthesized the data available on the long-term impacts of childhood abuse and neglect. Although research on several forms of child abuse is still quite limited, it seems clear that untreated trauma arising from abuse during childhood constitutes a major risk factor for a variety of mental health and social problems later in life. The implications of this relationship are substantial. They suggest that some significant proportion of the psychological and psychosocial difficulties of adolescents and adults are directly attributable to childhood maltreatment, despite the fact that most theories of psychopathology make no reference to child abuse in their analysis of etiology or their prescriptions regarding therapy.

When seen in its entirety, this review might appear to imply that the majority of psychological complaints presented by mental health clients or patients are based upon early childhood maltreatment. This impression is understandable, given that it more or less represents the author's view—at least once one takes into account the impacts of other relevant stressors such as recent victimization (e.g., PTSD in a rape victim or combat veteran), biologically mediated phenomena (e.g., schizophrenia or bipolar affective disorder), and the diffuse effects of an often injurious social system (e.g., the impacts of sexism, racism, or poverty). In fact, if the writings of cognitive, behavioral, and psychodynamic theorists are examined closely, it appears that they, too, implicate childhood maltreatment in the etiology of many psychological difficulties. This unanimity is not always clear, however, since these theorists rarely refer to child abuse per se. Nevertheless, most modern theories of nonpsychotic "psychopathology" would not predict adult symptomatology in an individual who was well treated and nurtured during childhood.

❑ Notes

1. A second, more common, motivation for self-mutilation is discussed later in this chapter.

2. A 1990 *Los Angeles Times* article, for example, presented the views of an authority on codependency who reportedly told a conference of women ministers, "My experience is that everybody in this audience is an addict of some kind or another." Among the potential addictions the speaker reportedly referred to were those to television, relationships, food, gambling, shopping, romance, nicotine, caffeine, alcohol, drugs, sex, and work (Krier, 1990, p. E1).

3. Although such activity is often called *promiscuous*, this term has blaming (and often sexist) connotations—for example, of "loose, immoral, [and] licentious" behavior (Lewis, 1978, p. 326)—and thus will not be used in this book.

PART III

EXPLORING THE SOLUTION ABUSE-FOCUSED PSYCHOTHERAPY

The remaining chapters of this book describe a psychotherapy for adult survivors of childhood abuse. The intent is to present a general approach to abuse-focused treatment, rather than a set of rigidly prescribed techniques or a programmatic system of interventions. Because there is less research available on the treatment of abuse effects, this section necessarily cites fewer studies or established authorities. Instead, the following chapters draw more centrally on the recent writings of abuse-specializing clinicians (e.g., Briere, 1989; Courtois, 1988; Gil, 1988; Meiselman, 1990), and on those implications for treatment that logically follow from the material presented in Chapters 2 and 3.

Additional information is available on various treatment procedures that have proved helpful with related problems: the value of catharsis, support, and normalization in assisting victims of other forms of trauma; cognitive therapies that have proved helpful with situationally related depression; behavioral interventions shown to be efficacious for anxiety; and psychodynamic methodologies that seek to address the sequelae of early developmental disruption, loss, or abandonment. This material must not be overlooked merely because it has not been developed in the context of abuse-related issues. At the same time, however, rarely will it be appropriate to accept all the assumptions or tenets of any given approach as they specifically apply to child abuse trauma.

4

Philosophy of Treatment

This chapter outlines an overall philosophy of treatment relevant to adults abused as children. Although clinical theory and techniques are an important component of abuse-focused psychotherapy, at least as important to successful outcome is the therapist's general orientation to working with abuse survivors. For example, a clinician who uses some of the methods described in Chapter 6 but who tends to pathologize his or her clients or deprive them of self-determination is unlikely to be especially helpful. On the other hand, a clinician whose approach validates and supports the client's experience may be successful in assisting survivors, to some extent regardless of the specific therapeutic techniques she or he employs during treatment.

❏ Respect, Positive Regard, and the Assumption of Growth

A central aspect of abuse-focused psychotherapy is the recognition that adults abused as children are *survivors*—individuals who have persevered despite often extreme childhood trauma and later abuse-related difficulties. This appreciation of the strength (rather than pathology) implicit in survivorhood underlies much of the philosophy of treatment in this area, primarily in terms of the respectful, positive stance required of the therapist. As opposed to certain more traditional mental health perspectives, abuse-focused therapy suggests that the client is not mentally ill or suffering from a defect, but rather is an individual whose life has been shaped, in part, by ongoing adaptation to a toxic environment. Thus the goal of therapy is less the survivor's recovery than his or her continued growth and development—an approach that utilizes the survivor's already existing skills to move beyond his or her current level of adaptive functioning. This point is well made by Sandra Butler in her preface to *Therapy for Adults Molested as Children*:

> For many survivors, the healing process is a battle of reclamation, of redirecting growth from the deeply gnarled roots of childhood. In my own work with survivors, I call this the "celebration of scar tissue." While there is often deep scarring, the survivor is much more than a collection of wounds. She is also resilient and resourceful. The scar tissue is what remains of the ways in which she protected herself, distanced or withdrew if needed, denied, forgot, minimized, sealed off. The scars are what allowed the survivor to reach our office or agency so that we might join her as she continues to heal. (in Briere, 1989, p. xii)

It has been suggested by some clinicians that such a perspective, while uplifting, overlooks the extremity of the damage done to some adults abused as children. Among the abuse effects pointed to in this regard are the "impaired object relations" of some survivors, and the extent of interpersonal problems and self-destructiveness sometimes present. Although it is true that child abuse can have severe impacts, it is important to note both the adaptive components of many aspects of severe interpersonal dysfunction, and the fact that such individuals possess, by definition, the extensive skills and capacities that have ensured their continued existence into adulthood. Thus the critical issue may be less whether abuse trauma can be extreme than the fact that the central process in survivorhood is continued adaptation, survival, and growth despite such injuries—

processes that the clinician can call upon in her or his work with former child abuse victims.

The pathology-focused stance sometimes described as *clinical objectivity* by certain psychotherapists directly and indirectly conveys to the survivor a number of disconfirming messages, including the following (overstated in the interests of clarification):

> You have a disorder, a psychological lesion, deficiencies and excesses —your life has made you less than others, for which you require treatment. The treatment you require must be controlled by an expert such as myself—if you were qualified to help yourself, you would be in better shape right now. You and I are beings of different types—although I can understand you by virtue of my clinical training, I am certainly not at all like you. You are not trustworthy—I must keep my distance from you or else you will seduce/entrap/contaminate me.

Ultimately, abuse-focused psychotherapy sends a different message:

> You have spent much of your life struggling to survive what was done to you as a child. The solutions you've found for the fear, emptiness, and memories you carry represent the best you could do in the face of the abuse you experienced. Although some others, perhaps even you, see your coping behaviors as sick or "dysfunctional," your actions have been the reverse: healthy accommodations to a toxic environment. Because you are not sick, therapy is not about a cure—it is about survival at a new level, about even better survival. Your job is to marshal your courage, to go back to the frightening thoughts and images of your childhood, and to update your experience of yourself and the world. My job, the easier of the two, is to engineer an environment where you can do this important work, and to provide in our sessions the safety and respect that you deserve.

❑ The Phenomenological Perspective

Much of modern mental health practice is predicated on the value of assigning a diagnosis and applying a treatment theoretically appropriate to the identified disorder. This approach often works well in medicine, and can be helpful in those aspects of psychiatry where diagnosis and treatment address organic factors (e.g., the use of neuroleptic medication in the treatment of schizophrenia). In work with abuse survivors, however, this approach is problematic.

Because most mental health theory has been developed almost entirely without reference to child abuse or its effects, traditional diagnosis and treatment of abuse survivors usually overlooks or misinterprets various aspects of postabuse trauma, leading to potentially inadequate or even destructive interventions. This problem is exacerbated by the fact that early trauma often causes abused children's development to branch off from the usual sequence, producing individuals whose psychologies are, in some sense, less easily understood by theories based on more typical development. Given the resultant poor fit between survivor experience and mental health theory, the therapist must return to the client for much of the information he or she needs to guide effective treatment.

Additionally, by virtue of their emphasis on cognitive tasks such as assignment of diagnostic labels and the application of abstract theoretical principles to the survivor's presenting symptoms, classical clinical perspectives can support the clinician's ongoing dissociation from the survivor during therapy, a process that almost inevitably reduces empathy and understanding. In its most unfortunate incarnation, this manifests in needlessly analytic, sometimes misguided, therapist behavior. In the words of one survivor, "I couldn't talk to her because she acted too much like a therapist. I felt like a bug under a magnifying glass. When she started telling me what I was thinking I had to leave."

While not ignoring the value of ongoing assessment, or the use of appropriate (i.e., abuse-relevant) theory as a guide to treatment, the current perspective emphasizes the benefits of a phenomenological view during psychotherapy. In this context, *phenomenology* refers to the survivor's personal experiences and perceptions as an important criterion for therapeutic actions, rather than sole reliance on theoretical notions that may or may not fit the survivor's experience. Thus, for example, whereas one clinician might interpret a survivor's self-mutilating behavior between sessions as an attempt to act out hostile and dependent feelings toward the therapist, a phenomenologic approach might lead the therapist to investigate directly why, in fact, the client engages in such behavior. As a result, perhaps, while the first clinician finds herself analyzing the survivor's resistance to interpretation, the second might learn that self-mutilation, for this client, serves as a tension-reduction response to the flashbacks and memories stimulated by the process of treatment. The widely disparate views of reality arising from these two approaches would have considerable implications for future therapy sessions.

A phenomenological therapeutic stance is necessarily empathic, since one of the therapist's most powerful tools becomes his or her ability to inhabit partially the survivor's inner world, and to perceive indirectly what the survivor perceives. This endeavor not only allows the therapist to offer accurately empathic statements, but assists with the process of treatment. By monitoring the survivor's internal state, via questions and attempts to understand his or her experience, for example, the clinician is less likely to move faster or slower in treatment than the client is able to go, and is more able to communicate in a manner most congruent with the client's subjective understanding of self and others. Further, to the extent that the clinician is attuned to the client's phenomenology, he or she is more likely to focus on issues most critical to the survivor, rather than being distracted by less important themes or dynamics.

❏ Functionality of "Symptoms" and Defenses

Implicit in the abuse perspective outlined in these chapters is the notion that what some see as dysfunctional survivor behavior is usually the logical and psychological extension of survivors' childhood experiences: reflective of their accommodations to early victimization and/or their responses to later abuse-related distress. There are several clinical implications of this perspective.

1. Because such behavior is or was adaptive, it is inherently pragmatic rather than symptomatic. In other words, the behaviors in question are not passive symptoms of some greater disturbance, but instead usually reflect the client's ongoing attempts to do what the therapist would have him or her do: cope and

respond to the environment as effectively as possible. The dysfunctional component of such behavior thus rests not in its form (e.g., manipulation or self-mutilation), but rather in the abuse-related assumptions or perceptions that motivate its appearance (e.g., expectations of abandonment or maltreatment) and the internal states that support it (e.g., emptiness or extreme dysphoria). Thus the goal of treatment ceases to be solely the removal of any given set of symptoms, but also the updating of abuse-distorted assumptions and the resolution of abuse-related trauma.

2. Because such behavior serves a psychological purpose, it is not easily given up by the survivor. For example, the former abuse victim whose substance abuse blocks painful memories and flashbacks is unlikely to stop smoking cocaine in the presence of continuing posttraumatic symptomatology. Similarly, the client whose indiscriminate sexual activity arises from a strong need for interpersonal attention or soothing will rarely stop such behavior in response to therapist entreaties or fear of disease. Awareness of the functionality of many survivor behaviors thus may protect the therapist from unnecessary preoccupation with client resistance or from wasting time trying somehow to convince the survivor of the illogic of her or his behavior. Instead, the clinician is counseled to avoid what the former abuse victim views as antisurvival suggestions or admonitions (e.g., "Just say no to drugs" or "You've got to promise me you won't cut on yourself anymore") in the absence of either (a) a change in whatever is addressed by the behavior or (b) new, more effective coping strategies.

3. Because such behavior reflects responses to real-world events, the clinician can be informed by "symptomatic" client activities. They offer data regarding both (a) what the survivor's early life must have been like, such that the behaviors in question were logical adaptive responses, and (b) what the client's current experience must be, such that she or he engages in these early behaviors now, during adulthood. As suggested by the phenomenological view described earlier, it is often only through a true appreciation of the client's immediate motiva-

tion for seemingly dysfunctional behavior that the clinician can truly understand the survivor's day-to-day experience without pathologizing it.

Ultimately, the clinician's understanding of the defensive and adaptive aspects of symptomatic behavior allows him or her to identify more clearly the underlying cognitive and affective sequelae of the client's childhood history, and thus to envision more accurately the actual targets of treatment. Without such a view, therapy may easily become misdirected toward superficial outcomes and/or inappropriate goals.

❑ Awareness and Integration

One of the ironies of abuse-focused psychotherapy is its requirement that the client approach a state he or she has spent much of life avoiding: integrated awareness of the present and the past, of previously split off or compartmentalized internal experience. Through dissociation, avoidance, denial, and other defensive strategies, the survivor can devote considerable psychological resources to the reduction of abuse-related pain—primarily by disintegrating and narrowing conscious awareness. The underlying motive for this response can be paraphrased as "What I don't know can't hurt me" or "Ignorance may not be bliss, but it is less painful than realization."

Abuse-focused therapy endorses an entirely different set of principles. It assumes that greater awareness of the past and present allows the survivor to discover and address the basis of his or her discontent. It further assumes that this process in some sense reworks the client's early reactions to trauma by providing adult-level insight into the "whys" and "whats" of the victimization, as opposed to the retained cognitive reactions and impressions of an injured child. This understanding promotes the survivor's developing self-acceptance, and assists in his or her rejection of the myth of personal badness. Additionally, the therapeutic reexperiencing of previously dissociated traumatic events *without* significant dissociation provides the survivor with an important opportunity to process abuse-relevant affects (e.g., fear, sadness, anger) and to develop a new relationship to his or her internal experience.

Among the tasks inherent in the process of reworking abuse-period affects is the survivor's growing ability to experience simultaneous contradictory feelings (e.g., anger and love, or fear and rage) without defensively dampening one and intensifying the other or rapidly alternating between the two. The client's growing ability to experience painful events directly without reflexive dissociation also allows greater psychological functioning in the "here and now," where problem solving and adjustment are usually preferable to defensive avoidance.

This divergence between client and therapist agendas, especially early in therapy, often results in a figurative battleground: The clinician invites the survivor to truly see and understand, while the survivor struggles to avoid what she or he believes to be dangerous awareness. This conflict has at least two implications for therapy:

1. From the client's perspective, therapy is not necessarily a straightforward process of learning and understanding. Instead, it often represents an ongoing, distressing contradiction: "Give up your defenses and survival strategies, confront painful memories and their implications, in order to survive better and hurt less." Given this perspective, the therapist may better understand client resistance or acting out as, instead, the client's sometimes desperate reliance on previously effective coping strategies in the face of a very frightening process —attempts, in fact, to survive therapy psychologically.

2. In light of the seemingly dangerous expectations and goals of psychotherapy, the client's willingness to continue treatment and somehow trust the therapy process is an act of extraordinary bravery. This courage should be directly acknowledged by the therapist—such recognition not only reassures the client that the clinician is aware of the arduousness of the therapy process for the survivor, but also helps the clinician to develop and maintain the respect and supportiveness required of those who work with former child abuse victims.

❑ The Therapeutic Structure

Because child abuse inherently involves violation of physical and/ or psychological integrity, the survivor may grow to expect invasion in a variety of other relationships—especially those involving intimacy or unequal power. Additionally, as noted in previous chapters, early abuse appears to disrupt the formation of a complete sense of self. Lacking integrated self-awareness, survivors may have difficulty discriminating their own issues, needs, and entitlements from those of others, with resultant boundary confusion.

Given the above, psychotherapy with abuse survivors must directly address the structural parameters of the therapeutic relationship—that is, that the client has the right to safety, self-regard, and self-determination; that neither the therapist nor the client can intrude where he or she is not allowed; and that both therapist and client are prohibited from turning the therapeutic relationship into a sexual, romantic, or exploitive one. The system of rules and limits that allows client vulnerability and intimacy, yet safety and self-determination, is held to be integral to successful treatment. Generally, these parameters ensure the uniqueness of the therapeutic relationship, wherein the sole task of interaction is the growth and development of the client, as opposed to the bidirectionality inherent in relationships where both parties' needs are addressed. This notion that psychotherapy is for the client, not the therapist, is often hard for the survivor to apprehend—especially given his or her experience with exploitive relationships in the past.

These structural elements have important implications for the survivor. First, they work to reassure her or him that, by the nature of the injunctions that bind both clinician and client, therapy will not recapitulate the violation, betrayal, or danger of the original abuse dynamic. Second, they define the outer limits of the treatment relationship, so that the survivor knows what he or she can expect (e.g., support, respect, and safety) and what is impossible to obtain (e.g., romantic love, sex, or overinvolvement in the therapist's personal life). Finally, they offer a sense of containment—by defining the parameters of treatment, they provide a reliable, predictable environment from which the survivor can safely interact with the therapist and confront upsetting memories or feelings.

Although the client may at times struggle against these strictures (for example, demanding a personal relationship with the therapist, or castigating the clinician for being rigid or withholding when he or she insists on "the rules"), the intent of the therapeutic structure includes the survivor's growing awareness of boundaries when interacting with others. Most important, the client observes the therapist's respect for him or her, manifest in the clinician's avoidance of coercive or exploitive interpersonal behaviors, and the therapist's support for the client's fledgling attempts to understand his or her entitlements as a human being. Additionally, the client observes the therapist's ability to resist the pressure of the client's inappropriate demands, and/or the client's attempts to violate the therapist's boundaries. Over time, this growing atmosphere of mutual respect and boundary delimitation can serve as an antidote to the survivor's childhood experiences, where the opposite dynamics frequently pertained.

❏ Therapy as Reality Based

As noted in Chapter 3, a considerable proportion of survivors' abuse-related difficulties lie in the interpersonal domain. Not only did child abuse teach survivors that human connections are dangerous and fraught with conflict, it altered their perceptions of and response to power, intimacy, and relationships. One effect of this process is survivors' tendency to project or transfer abuse-based understanding and cognitive defenses onto the therapist and the clinical relationship. As a result, survivors' perceptions of therapy may reflect an amalgam of early experience and more immediate reality. For example, a client may view the therapist as, in part, abuserlike, and thus respond to her or him with fear or anger, or with behaviors expected in the original abusive relationship. Later in therapy there may be a tendency for the survivor to fantasize the clinician as an all-powerful rescuer—the one the survivor so deeply hoped for as an abused child—who will bestow a magic cure and/or fill the client's emptiness. The fantasy may be romantic: The therapist and client may be cast as a heroic dyad, united in their battle against the world and the survivor's history. Or the therapist may be fantasized as a special friend who, but for the constraints of treatment, would gladly be a partner or lover. The clinician may become as much a representative of what the client fears or desires as any real person, motivating behaviors during treatment that are, in some sense, symbolic and far removed from the actual therapeutic situation.

It should be noted that this sense of unreality does not reflect a pathological state, but rather arises from the conditions under which the abuse took place (e.g., secrecy, violation, deprivation, misrepresentation) and the intensity and intimacy of the therapeutic environment. As a result, the therapy relationship is influenced by projection and fantasy. An important aspect of abuse-focused psychotherapy is therefore the therapist's gentle but steadfast insistence on reality-based interactions, to the extent that they can be tolerated by the client. This reality, of course, is technically illusive—both the client and the therapist bring to the session their own experiences, assumptions, and expectations that color interpersonal perception. Despite this subjectivity, the focus of psychotherapy should be on understanding, clarification, and awareness—the increasing ability of the client to view self and others without blinders. In aid of this process, the clinician must work to keep the therapeutic relationship based in reality, rather than a recapitulation of the distortions and dissociations present in the original abuse dynamic or the fantasies that the survivor marshaled in order to cope with maltreatment or exploitation.

This focus does not mean, however, that the clinician rejects or derides the client's transference, internal representations of reality, or need to use fantasy to inject optimism or safety into the difficult task of therapy. Rather, it informs the clinician about the importance of his or her own behavior, and reinforces that it must be honest, unambiguous, and relentlessly invested in the client's growth and increased awareness.

It is in this domain that traditional psychodynamic practice offers the therapeutic interpretation: gentle, carefully timed suggestions to the client regarding what the therapist believes to be the basis for the client's behavior. Abuse-focused therapy may also involve interpretation, primarily in terms of making connections between current problems and childhood experiences, but more typically avoids telling the client what is true. Among other problems with overuse of this approach, therapist statements about reality are likely to be, at best, somewhat inaccurate, and thus ironically supportive of unreality. Further, because interpretations are, by definition, not yet part of the client's understanding or belief system, they may be perceived as false and/or disconfirming—as yet another example of others trying to coerce, lie to, or control the survivor. Finally, by virtue of the power invested in informing the client about what he or she believes to be true, the clinician unwittingly reinforces a fantasy: that the clinician is especially wise and competent and can be counted upon to give important answers that the survivor otherwise could not obtain. The potentially destructive aspect of this fantasy is the other side of the myth: that the survivor is less able to help him- or herself than actually may be the case.

Rather than overreliance on interpretation to inject accurate awareness into the therapeutic process, the clinician may find it more helpful to encourage the client's own discovery of important personal truths. Perhaps most useful, in this regard, is *Socratic therapy:* the clinician's frequent, gentle use of questions to facilitate the survivor's understanding. As opposed to closed-ended inquiries that require mere yes or no answers, the therapist asks carefully timed questions that stimulate exploration, such as, What do you think all of this means? What just happened? Why do you think you had to cut on yourself when you remembered that? What did you think my reaction was going to be? Why do you think you did that? What are you feeling right now? Although the survivor may respond to such questions early in therapy as if they were interrogations, hidden statements, or covert demands for certain responses, the clinician's actual interest in the client's answers and her or his manifest absence of judgment eventually provide the client with the opportunity to sort out important issues in the context of therapist support.

The clinician also can encourage reality-based interactions by not joining the client in fantasy. It is not uncommon, in this regard, for the therapist to want to act as protector, parent, special friend, or deity. These roles can reflect both the client's expressed need for a special relationship or an all-powerful guide and protector and the clinician's need to be special, talented, powerful, and needed. Despite such pressures, it is exactly during these scenarios that the clinician has the opportunity to produce change: Through studied noninvolvement in fantasies, the therapist can offer the more lasting benefits of a reality-based relationship. In some sense, the communication is as follows:

> I understand your desire to have a special relationship with me, one that meets your needs for connectedness, rescue, protection, even love. But our relationship isn't for those things. It's better, because it's based on you and your continued learning and growth—not on a fantasy that could be blown away in a second (as undoubtedly it has many times in your past). Because it is real, you can count on it, on me. The good news is that although I am not your fantasized savior/parent/lover, this relationship *is* a place where you can feel safe, supported, and optimistic, and where you can examine things that you otherwise might not. All of these things are based upon what is actually present, right now, right here.

One result of effective abuse-focused treatment is the client's slow de-idealization of the clinician, without concomitant devaluation or dysphoria. The psychotherapist ceases to become the only valid and good person in the world, his or her assessments and impressions become less central to the survivor's well-being, and his or her humanity becomes less threatening. Implicit in this process is the survivor's decreasing need for the therapeutic relationship to be unreal, based on both a growing awareness of the positive aspects of healthy relatedness and the decreased power of abuse-based needs and perceptions in the survivor's current life.

❑ Social Context

Because it deals specifically with victims of socially prevalent violence, abuse-focused psychotherapy must confront the sociocultural context of the abuse survivor's distress. By considering social as well as personal dynamics, this perspective adds to the clinician's understanding of how his or her clients came to be the way they are, both in terms of their adjustment to toxic childhood environments and the interventions necessary to assist them in resolving injury not of their own making.

The cultural aspects of child abuse are, at minimum, threefold. First, broad social forces support or allow the victimization of those with lesser social power, resulting in high rates of child maltreatment. The social component of sexual abuse is suggested by a recent study in which it was found that significant numbers of nonclinical, nonincarcerated males are interested in sexual contact with children (Briere & Runtz, 1989b). Of 193 male undergraduate students in the study sample, 21% described sexual attraction to at least some small children, 9% admitted to sexual fantasies involving children, and 7% indicated some likelihood of having sex with a child if they could avoid detection and punishment. Similar numbers, primarily in terms of sexual attraction to small children, were reported in another male university sample by Smiljanich (1992). The presence of so many pedophilic-like individuals in relatively high-functioning, "normal" samples supports the notion that the sexualization of children is at least partially a social phenomenon.

Second, there appear to be socially transmitted attitudes and beliefs that deny or minimize the implications and impacts of child abuse (Summit, 1988). Briere, Henschel, and Smiljanich (in press), for example, found that a significant minority of university students at least partially endorsed statements such as "Many children would like sex with an adult once they tried it," "Children sometimes try to seduce adults," and "Sex with children is relatively harmless." Agreement with such statements was associated with self-reported use of pornography, endorsement of sexual aggression against women, greater levels of sexual activity, being male, and, most important, self-reported willingness to abuse a child sexually in the absence of detection or punishment.

Finally, there are often negative social reactions to the abuse survivor's subsequent behavior, based on his or her deviation from social norms regarding appropriate conduct. This often takes the form of victim blaming by clinicians and others, who may especially question the credibility or importance of survivors' abuse reports. Several studies indicate that mental health professionals tend to hold attitudes that underestimate the frequency and impacts of sexual abuse, view molestation more as a symptom of a pathogenic family system than as a directly traumatic event, and/or discount abuse disclosures as fantasies or memory distortions (e.g., Eisenberg, Owens, & Dewey, 1987; Finkelhor, 1984; LaBarbera, Martin, & Dozier, 1980). For example, the sexual abuse survivor whose childhood injury has led to "histrionic" or "borderline" behavior may be assumed to be exaggerating or lying about childhood molestation in order to focus attention on him- or herself, and/or may be seen as a seductive or masochistic person who seeks out sexual or physical victimization. The survivor's supposed desire for abuse, in fact, may be invoked to explain why he or she was victimized in the first place. An especially blatant example of this phenomenon is the writing of Henderson (1975), who states in the *Comprehensive Textbook of Psychiatry*:

> The daughters collude in the incestuous liaison and play an active and even initiating role in establishing the pattern. . . . [The daughter] is unlikely to report the liaison at first or protest about it. If she eventually does, it is as much precipitated by anger at her father for something else . . . as a real objection to his incestuous behavior. (p. 1356)

Given this social context, it is not surprising that many abuse survivors inappropriately assume responsibility for what was done to them as children, perhaps deny that abuse ever occurred in the first place, and underestimate their personal rights to self-determination and safety. This internalization of society's abuse-supportive beliefs, with resultant guilt, shame, and self-blame, becomes an important target for abuse-focused therapy—one that may be overlooked by more traditional psychotherapies.

By including social factors in his or her therapeutic formulations, the clinician may support the survivor in accomplishing at least three important treatment goals:

1. greater insight into aspects of the abuse that, by definition, do not relate to intrapsychic dynamics
2. redirection of abuse-related anger from self to perpetrator and society, leading to a concomitant reduction in self-punitive thoughts and feelings
3. the development of self-perceptions less based upon conformity to destructive cultural beliefs and more reflective of self-acceptance and self-determination

More broadly, a social perspective directs the clinician's attention away from pathology-based interpretations that stress individual weakness or dysfunction. Instead, the survivor is seen as someone whose adverse life experiences have blocked optimal development, but who has struggled, nevertheless, to adapt to harsh external contingencies. From this perspective, the survivor's "disturbed" behavior may more accurately be seen as reflecting the injuriousness of his or her social environment than as evidence of any inherent personal deficits or failings. Becker, Lira, Castillo, Gomez, and Kovalskys (1990) present a similar argument, although in a different arena:

> As the events of suffering are communicated in the therapeutic context, they cease being solely private experiences that are best forgotten, and become indictments of the social context. . . . For example, during a "day of protest" [in Chile] in 1983, a woman let her son leave the house to watch television with the neighbors. While crossing the street, he was shot by a police squad. When the mother came to therapy, she was experiencing an extremely altered grief process because she felt guilty for the death of her son. Therapy had to be the place where she learned that her son was shot as part of mass political repression, and that her private and personal loss was caused by a sociopolitical situation. To mourn productively, she needed our concern and protection, but she also needed to understand the political aspects of the problem. (p. 143)

❏ **Summary**

This chapter has outlined a number of philosophical issues implicit in abuse-focused psychotherapy. It is suggested that optimal therapy for child abuse trauma requires unwavering attention to the inner experience of the survivor, understanding of the social context of victimization, and a treatment perspective that views "symptomatic" survivor behaviors as logical responses to posttraumatic learning, cognitions, and affects. The importance of respect for the survivor has been emphasized, both in terms of the courage and strength inherent in his or her perseverance despite significant injury and based upon the notion that human dignity and self-determination are necessary conditions for optimal psychological functioning. The following three chapters attempt to build on this basic foundation by presenting more specific therapeutic suggestions and perspectives.

5

Parameters of Treatment I: Process Issues

As is probably true for any longer-term psychotherapeutic process, what happens in a given abuse-focused therapy session is often more important than the specific content of what is said. Thus, for example, an occasion of therapist support can be more helpful than a specific clinical interpretation, and a client's act of struggling with a painful memory may be even more significant than what, in fact, the memory contains. As a result, the interaction between client and therapist becomes paramount, as does the ebb and flow of the therapy session.

Among those areas in which therapeutic "process" is especially important in abuse-focused therapy are the following:

- the role and timing of assessment
- the balance between exploration of potentially distressing material and the need to provide support and consolidation
- intensity control

98

- decisions about when to focus on present concerns versus historical events
- the negotiation of client "resistance"
- the sequence in which problems are addressed in relation to "self" versus "trauma"
- termination issues

❑ Assessment

It is an axiom of most psychotherapeutic approaches that assessment must precede treatment. Obviously, in order to assist someone with a problem, one must have some understanding of what the problem is. Such information is especially important in work with abuse survivors, whose difficulties are likely to involve multiple areas of psychosocial functioning. It is exactly this complexity of postabuse trauma, however, that makes assessment an ongoing process throughout therapy, rather than an isolated, pretreatment procedure. As noted by Steer (1988), for example, details of the survivor's abuse history may be repressed at the onset of psychotherapy, such that a true appraisal of the individual's childhood experience may not be possible until well into the treatment process. Similarly, Courtois (1988), Gelinas (1983), and others note that aspects of the survivor's psychological status may be masked or disguised early in therapy as a result of the client's need to dissociate from painful experience. Thus assessment and treatment may become essentially indistinguishable as therapy unfolds and the survivor is increasingly able to confront and express her or his internal world.

Assessment, whether at the onset of treatment or during therapy, ideally addresses at least two domains: (a) the survivor's current knowledge of his or her childhood history, and (b) the survivor's currently experienced symptoms, problems, and affects relative to his or her strengths, capacities, and resources. Information in these areas not only provides the clinician with needed feedback regarding targets for intervention and (to some extent) the progress of therapy, it also offers data on the appropriate pace and content of the therapeutic interaction. If the therapist determines that the

survivor is experiencing intrusive symptoms and deepening dysphoria, for example, he or she is less likely to focus the current session on uncovering further abuse memories than if the client presents as relatively stable and able to devote energy to exploration.

ABUSE HISTORY

It is widely held among trauma-specialized clinicians that survivors of severe abuse usually come to psychotherapy with incomplete memory of their maltreatment. Certain especially injurious,
humiliating, or distressing victimization experiences can be at least
partially repressed, only entering complete conscious awareness as
therapy progresses, dissociation diminishes, and/or environmental
events restimulate them (Courtois, in press). Because abuse-focused
therapy repeatedly addresses abuse memories, the clinician usually
has relatively up-to-date information on what the survivor currently knows about his or her victimization. Nevertheless, it is often
helpful to "check in" periodically with the survivor regarding his
or her current memories of childhood maltreatment.

Information on abuse experiences assists the therapist in at least
two areas. First, knowledge of abuse type and severity allows the
clinician to predict, to some extent, the types of problems with which
the survivor may be struggling. One would expect, for example,
that a woman who was raped by a tyrannical, rageful father might
present with (at minimum) problems in the areas of trust, boundaries, sexuality, authority, and strong emotions from others. Second,
knowing the ways in which the client was hurt as a child can inform
the therapist of potential transferential and conditioned responses
that might occur during treatment. For example, a client who was
repeatedly derogated and verbally assaulted in childhood might be
especially sensitive to real or implied criticism, and thus might best
respond to therapist feedback that is couched in especially nonjudgmental language. Similarly, the clinician working with a sexual
abuse survivor might choose to be especially explicit about therapeutic boundaries, and might be even more careful than usual to
avoid any actions or statements that could be interpreted as sexual
or seductive.

PSYCHOLOGICAL STATE

A cornerstone of effective abuse focused psychotherapy is ongo ing evaluation of the client's current internal experience. As indicated in Chapter 4, a phenomenological approach requires the therapist to be as attuned as possible to the survivor's immediate feeling state, as well as to the relative presence or absence of intrusive memories, thoughts, and images. Unfortunately, such information is difficult to obtain from some abuse survivors, who may have learned to attenuate or to avoid painful internal experiences through the use of dissociation, denial, and/or "as if" defenses (Briere, 1989). It is a common error of both beginning and experienced therapists to misinterpret a neutral or seemingly positive demeanor and reported absence of painful affect as evidence that the survivor is doing well. As a result, the clinician may become less vigilant to what is actually considerable pain, an impending crisis, or the beginnings of an episode of self-destructiveness. Additionally, the survivor's cheerful or casual facade may lead the therapist to move faster in treatment than is appropriate, and/or to terminate psychotherapy well before it is indicated.

Although there are no hard-and-fast rules about the assessment of affective avoidance, clinicians may find it helpful to ask themselves some version of the following questions:

- Does the client's current emotional presentation make sense, based on what I know of her circumstances and history?
- Does the client's affect seem "deep" enough (is it responsive to therapeutic events, or is it more brittle and superficial than it has been or seemingly should be)?
- Is there evidence of significant dissociation (is the client's gaze fixed, has his voice become a monotone, are her verbalizations stilted or his phraseology uncharacteristic)?
- Are the client's facial or body movements either reduced or stereotyped?
- Does the client seem to be especially avoidant of certain topics, relative to previous sessions?
- What would I feel like right now if I were the client? Does this match what I'm seeing?

❑ **Exploration Versus Consolidation**

Richard

As described earlier, Richard is a physical abuse survivor who utilizes (among other things) drugs, alcohol, and sex to avoid memories and feelings associated with his abuse. He began his last session with reports of repetitive nightmares and intrusive thoughts of stabbing himself with a screwdriver. Soon into the session Richard yelled at his therapist and threw a box of tissues across the room. Although his psychologist felt that new abuse-related material might be moving into awareness, she decided that Richard was too overwhelmed to explore or process such material in any detail. Instead, she shared with him her impression that he was feeling "unsettled" by therapy and by his greater openness to his past, and noted that this might be a good time to work on ways he could calm himself (both acutely and in the near future) without turning to drugs or some other self-injurious behavior. In contrast to his previous outburst, Richard responded to the therapist's soothing approach and support for self-care with what appeared to be considerable relief.

To the extent that the client's internal state can be ascertained, perhaps the most important issue is whether to proceed with uncovering or exploratory work or to engage in further stabilization, reassurance, and support. Generally, abuse-focused clinicians have found it useful to weigh the extent of intrusive symptomatology (e.g., flashbacks or nightmares), level of dissociation, and extent of painful affect (e.g., anxiety, depression, or anger) against the client's available psychological resources or capacities. If the survivor appears to be in crisis, besieged by acute posttraumatic symptoms, or deeply dissociated, the decision is usually to focus on stabilization and support. During such times the clinician will refrain from exploring abuse recollections in depth or discussing especially painful topics in detail, and instead will validate and normalize the client's current experience, consolidate previous progress, and work with the client to increase feelings of safety and control. This less intensive work should not be presented as evidence of the client's weakness or pathology, but rather as normal manifestations of the ebb and flow of therapy and the therapist's appreciation of exactly how taxing and difficult grappling with abuse-related pain can be.

❏ Intensity Control Within the Session

The pace and focus of psychotherapy rests not only on the client's relative ability to tolerate additional stress at any given point in time, but also on the inherent structure of the session. To the extent that pacing is under the control of the therapist, the typical abuse-focused therapy session should begin at relatively low intensity, build to a peak around mid-session, and then gradually return to a base-line level by the session's end. On some occasions, of course, as when the client enters the session already in crisis or acute distress, there may be no reasonable way to avoid immediately high levels of pain ful affect. Such instances, however, especially require serious attempts to provide the client with some level of dearousal before the end of the session.

By not immediately jumping into affectively laden material, the therapist provides an environment where the survivor can establish safety and rapport, and then move at her or his own pace into more stressful or frightening domains. By slowly bringing the client back down to lower arousal levels by the end of the session, the clinician honors the survivor's (often unexpressed) need for control, closure, and composure prior to reentering the outside world. In addition, such activities encourage the development of affect regulation skills, as the survivor gradually learns how to deescalate affective tension by repeatedly moving from greater to lesser levels of emotional intensity.

Intensity control is especially crucial in reducing what others might view as acting out between sessions. It is likely that some instances of client self-mutilation, substance abuse, or indiscriminate sexual activity that occur soon after an intense psychotherapy session actually represent the survivor's use of tension-reduction devices to deal with therapy-restimulated abuse trauma. To the extent that therapy allows the survivor to find closure and to reconstitute his

or her defenses prior to leaving the therapeutic environment, the
need for later tension reduction may be correspondingly reduced.

❑   **Time Focus**

Because abuse trauma involves both the past (when the abuse
occurred) and the present (when long-term effects are experienced),
therapeutic intervention must logically take both into account. Yet
it is not always clear when to do which: At what point should the
therapist focus on the client's current problems, and when should
she or he delve into the client's childhood abuse experiences? It is
clear that limiting therapy to only one or the other is an error. The
therapist who devotes most of each session to immediate client
crises and difficulties, for example, may discover that she or he is
spending the majority of time "stamping out brushfires," without
having the opportunity to remediate the underlying, abuse-related
basis for these problems. Alternatively, the clinician who resolutely
restricts him- or herself to discussion of childhood issues and early
traumas runs the real risk of endangering the adult survivor's
immediate safety; by ignoring the crises and problems known to be
associated with a history of severe child abuse (e.g., dysfunctional
relationships, self-destructiveness, substance abuse), the therapist
is unable to monitor or intervene in the acute difficulties the client
may encounter as an adult.

In general, clinical experience suggests that effective work with
abuse trauma begins in the here and now, moves into the past—
when possible—during mid-session, then returns to the present at
session's end. This initial focus on current concerns serves at least
two purposes: It allows assessment of the survivor's current situation, state, and resources, and it typically provides a less intrusive
environment at treatment onset, as per the previous section on
intensity control.

For the client in acute distress, this strategy may result in entire
sessions in which immediate problems and issues are addressed,
without any exploration of earlier trauma. At the same time, however, the clinician monitors the process for evidence that, at mini-

mum, the client could tolerate some suggestion of links between current experiences and those he or she had as a child, if not formal exploration of childhood antecedents to the current situation. More commonly, however, the abuse survivor will present with periods of time, if not entire sessions, when current events and experiences are under sufficient control that direct attention to his or her childhood injuries is possible.

❏ Addressing Client "Resistance"

Implicit in several of the process issues presented in this chapter is the notion that the survivor's behavior in treatment has a logical, adaptive basis. Yet it is not uncommon for therapists to voice concern about clients' "resistance" to therapeutic intervention—implying that such individuals are intentionally engaging in obstructive behavior, to the detriment of their progress in treatment. As Freud (1958) muses in *A General Introduction to Psychoanalysis*, "To think that the patient, whose symptoms cause him and those around him such suffering, who is willing to make such sacrifices in time, money, effort, and self-conquest in order to be freed from them,—that he should, in the interests of his illness, resist the help offered him" (p. 297). Such client "illogic" is often invoked as an explanation for various negative therapeutic outcomes, ranging from client hostility to premature termination.

An abuse-focused perspective offers an alternative explanation for many "resistant" survivor behaviors, one that takes into account former abuse victims' hard-earned survival skills and, in many cases, their own accurate assessments of their current tolerance for therapy-specific events and affects. In fact, client "resistance" often constitutes feedback to the therapist regarding clinical process issues. The ultimate message inherent in client lateness for sessions, obvious avoidance of emotional experience or expression, failure to do therapy homework, or sudden disengagement during treatment, for example, may be "You're going too fast," "I'm not ready for this," or "You frighten me when you talk about that."

Thus the appropriate response to client "resistance" is often adjustment of the therapist's—not the client's—behavior. Most typically this involves one or more of the following:

- evaluation of the possibility that further work needs to be done on "self" issues, including the development of greater affect regulation skills, before this specific piece of work can be done
- evaluation of the psychological impact of the material being discussed (e.g., Could this particular memory or topic be more stressful or painful than the clinician had previously thought?)
- a resultant temporary decrease in the pace and/or intensity of therapy, thereby increasing the survivor's sense of control and reducing the possibility of affect overload
- a more indirect approach to whatever traumatic material appears to be stimulating such behavior, at least until the client appears to be better able to tolerate the associated distress
- greater attention to therapist-client safety and trust issues

Interestingly, client "resistance" does not inherently require that the therapist completely abandon exploration of the material at hand. For most clients, all that is necessary is greater attention to their needs for safety and self-determination, as balanced by equally important, judicious challenges to their trauma-based fear of awareness. Ultimately, the issue is a central one for abuse-focused therapy: What is the optimal level of exposure to potentially upsetting material that this client can tolerate without overwhelming his or her psychological defenses?

❑ Sequence of Therapeutic Goals

Because child abuse affects many areas of psychological functioning, it is not always clear what issue or problem should be addressed at what point in time. For example, which should early therapy focus on: distorted cognitions, posttraumatic flashbacks, depression, or impaired self-reference? Should these areas be approached in some sort of order—that is, does the successful treatment of certain problems require the prior resolution of others? Or, perhaps, should all of the survivor's presenting concerns be addressed more or less simultaneously?

As with other aspects of abuse-focused treatment, answers to these questions depend, to a large extent, on the extremity of the survivor's psychic injuries and his or her available resources. Clinical experience suggests that clients who have experienced very early and severe child abuse often suffer from basic impairments in self-relatedness and self-care, problems that may preclude their optimal response to treatment for other abuse-related difficulties. Thus, for example, the survivor who was emotionally neglected as an infant and then repeatedly sexually abused until her late teens is likely to have considerable difficulty with basic issues around affect regulation, self-support, self-definition, and adequate differentiation from her therapist and others—issues that will have to be addressed to some extent before she can effectively direct her attention to self-esteem problems or posttraumatic flashbacks (Courtois, 1991).

It is not uncommon, unfortunately, for therapists to focus prematurely on posttraumatic symptoms when, in fact, significant self problems await resolution. As a result, the clinician may report that "therapy is going nowhere," or, in a worse case, may describe escalating client disorganization as the survivor struggles to confront intrusive stimuli and painful affect without a stable internal base or sufficient affect regulation skills. The value of assessment in such instances becomes clear: Is the client prepared to address and explore childhood trauma directly, given that such reminiscence is, at best, unbalancing? Or is the client in need of basic "self work" (presented in the next chapter) before he or she can directly confront the pain of the past?

Interestingly, it is the author's experience that even the most injured of clients can tolerate some exploration of his or her trauma, and can participate to some extent in cognitive therapy—the critical issue appears to be the therapist's sensitivity to the shifting balance between internal resources and abuse-related pain experienced by the client at any given moment. Thus the therapist may choose to refer to a childhood beating while working with a client who is struggling to understand and define his boundaries in relation to others. Similarly, the survivor whose immediate task is to locate a fledgling sense of self may be responsive to feedback and suggestions regarding her reflexive self-derogation.

When self issues are not a major concern, as is true of many less injured abuse survivors, the sequence of therapeutic goals becomes more dependent on the type of abuse the client experienced as a child. Generally, sexual and physical abuse survivors profit from interventions that directly address posttraumatic symptoms or problems, whereas adults who were psychologically abused as children typically respond best to cognitive interventions that focus on self-esteem. In any work with survivors, however, the clinician must be prepared to shift approaches according to the immediate psychological state and needs of the client: focusing on trauma when indicated, then perhaps moving to an intervention addressing self-relatedness, then focusing on reassurance or a cognitive intervention before returning to trauma. Stated in another way, specific therapeutic techniques or approaches should be considered tools in abuse-specific therapy, not restrictive systems that interfere with the clinician's ability to assist the client's growth and development.

❑ Termination Issues

Despite its critical importance in the treatment process, the termination phase of psychotherapy is often overlooked by clinicians in their treatment planning. This neglect probably results from, among other things, the assumption that termination occurs naturally as a function of treatment success, as well as client (and/or therapist) discomfort about ending a gratifying, positive relationship.

The definition of positive therapeutic outcome eludes consensus, however. Some clinicians consider remission of some or all overt symptomatology to be a sufficient goal of psychotherapy, whereas others are more concerned with the resolution of "core" psychological issues and dynamics. Further, there may be disagreement between client and therapist about when either of these criteria have been met, let alone when treatment should be terminated.

The position taken in this book is that abuse-focused psychotherapy can be deemed entirely successful when (a) the abuse trauma underlying "symptomatology" and negative tension-reduction activities has been resolved, (b) abuse-relevant cognitive distortions no longer interfere with the client's daily functioning or reasonably positive self-perception, and (c) the survivor's access to self is sufficient to allow adequate self-support and a stable base from which to interact with others. For survivors of relatively severe childhood abuse who are engaged in optimal treatment, these goals require, at minimum, several years of therapy, and can entail substantially more.

"Entirely successful" therapy may exceed the resources or interests of many clients and some therapists, however. Citizens of the United States without sufficient finances or employment cannot pay for extended psychotherapy, for example, and most insurance companies and health maintenance organizations are not prepared to fund extensive treatment. Further, many individuals are unprepared to endure the discomfort of extended psychotherapy, or may not subscribe to a sociocultural perspective that endorses sitting in a room with another person at a given time, on a regular basis, for several years. For these reasons, it may be more appropriate to judge therapeutic outcome according to the manifest expectations or resources of the survivor. This constellation of needs, interests, and external supports might result in six months of symptom-based interventions for one survivor versus four years of "depth" psychotherapy for another.

Beyond successful outcome, however, a relatively separate issue is that of termination itself. Although the end of therapy may evolve intrinsically out of the treatment process in some instances, this is not necessarily the case for many abuse survivors. Because most child abuse trauma arises in the context of a primary relationship, the dissolution of the therapeutic dyad typically assumes greater proportions for the survivor and may, in fact, restimulate major abuse-related issues. Most notably, the end of treatment signals impending loss and the potential for perceived abandonment.

This mixture of "good news and bad news" means that termination issues must be carefully assessed and addressed before treatment can be considered complete. Among these issues are preparing for termination, dealing with restimulated loss and abandonment, and fears of regression.

PREPARATION FOR TERMINATION

Especially when therapy has been relatively long term, clients in abuse-focused therapy who do not independently bring up the issue require reasonable "warning" from the therapist that termination may soon be indicated. Ideally, this process will begin three to six months before therapy's end, and will represent some level of agreement between client and therapist regarding the appropriateness of termination in the not-too-distant future. By initiating this phase of treatment well before its end, the clinician provides the survivor with the opportunity to accommodate to the idea of termination per se, and to have sufficient time to process termination-specific reactions and affects.

RESTIMULATED TRAUMA, LOSS, AND ABANDONMENT ISSUES

Although treatment may have addressed the survivor's childhood history of separation, loss, and abandonment, these issues are likely to be restimulated by the process of ending therapy. As a result, it is not uncommon for the client to reexperience posttraumatic stress temporarily and even, in some instances, to fall back on earlier dissociative and tension-reduction defenses. The advantage of allocating considerable time to the termination phase of treatment is that this return of earlier feelings and responses can be normalized and dealt with in the same way any other restimulated material has been addressed during treatment. Thus termination work allows the client to access and process abuse-era experiences yet again, albeit now from the position of a stronger adult who is more experienced at addressing childhood pain and who has greater affective control and access to self-support.

FEARS OF POSTTREATMENT REGRESSION

Because successful abuse-focused treatment is often the context in which survivors experience their first major reduction in distress and, in some cases, where they "grow up" to substantially greater self-determination, a confusion may occur between therapy per se and the gains they have made. As a result, survivors may consciously or unconsciously fear that the end of therapy will be the end of their "new" selves. This fear can be compounded and reinforced by any resurgence in difficulties associated with the termination phase of treatment, as noted above.

Therapist response to regression fears consists primarily of reassurance. The client is gently reminded that therapy is where "getting better" took place, not the getting better itself. If this concern is of major proportions, the therapist may choose to stretch out termination by decreasing the number of sessions per unit of time, such as changing from twice to once a week. This gradual reduction in therapeutic contact not only allows the survivor to adjust to lesser therapeutic support, but demonstrates his or her sustained progress despite decreased interaction with the therapist.

❏ **Summary**

This brief chapter has outlined some of the primary process issues inherent in effective abuse-focused therapy. As noted at the outset, these and related principles are, at minimum, as important as the use of the specific interventions described in Chapter 6. Most generally, the process of therapy must balance two agendas: the survivor's need for safety, support, and stability and therapeutic processes that inherently stretch the survivor's capacities and admit threatening material into awareness. Interventions that focus too much on the former will slow the survivor's progress by not providing sufficient stimuli for growth, process desensitization, and the development of affect regulation skills. Clinicians who overuse the latter, on the other hand, run the very real risk of overstressing the survivor, a process that may cause the client (paradoxically) to withdraw and to take fewer healthy therapeutic risks, and may do actual harm by disrupting his or her normal adaptive capacities. How therapists handle the delicate and dynamic balance of these two competing needs is probably the best measure of their effectiveness as therapeutic resources for abuse survivors.

6

Parameters of Treatment II: Intervention Approaches

As noted in Chapters 2 and 3, child abuse effects range from post-traumatic stress and cognitive distortions to impaired self-reference. In light of the complexity of postabuse trauma, the psychotherapist must be prepared to address these problems with a correspondingly diverse set of therapeutic approaches. Further, since most current psychotherapeutic perspectives were developed without reference to childhood maltreatment, no one established treatment approach is likely to deal adequately with the long-term sequelae of child abuse. The treatment techniques outlined in this chapter therefore represent a combination of self-oriented, cognitive, and trauma-specific therapies, adapted to reflect the treatment philosophy outlined in Chapter 4.

☐ Intervening in Impaired Self-Reference

Marie

Marie has been in therapy for approximately eight months, addressing a childhood history of extensive emotional neglect by her mother and very early sexual abuse by one of her mother's boyfriends. Therapy has been difficult for Marie because of her constant fear that her therapist will somehow leave her, whether it be by death, job change, or deliberate abandonment. Because of these and other concerns, Marie phones or pages her therapist quite often, usually with some question or issue other than her actual need for reassurance and contact. Her therapist's stance at this point in treatment is to respond to her calls in a positive manner, although keeping all phone calls brief. His main communication to Marie thus far has been that she is safe with him, that he does not plan to leave her in the foreseeable future, and that her needs for reassurance are appropriate given her history and internal experience. Although she sometimes tests him with "fights" and boundary incursions, he refrains from significant confrontation or even major interpretations of her behavior, knowing that such responses would overwhelm her at the present time. He expects, however, that the development of a secure base at this point in time will allow Marie to take helpful therapeutic risks and tolerate more direct interventions later in treatment, and thus to grow beyond her current relationship with him and with herself.

Just as impaired self-reference is not easily defined, intervention in this area defies simple description. The goal of self work is to help the survivor build a positive source of identity, so that he or she is able to monitor internal states, call upon inner resources at times of stress, maintain internal coherence in interactions with others, and foster improved affect regulation. Among the complexities of such an endeavor are (a) the ethereal quality of the therapeutic target (How does one work with a phenomenon that is so difficult to identify?); (b) the fact that self-development occurs primarily in childhood, as opposed to later in life, and thus it is not always clear how to accomplish this task outside the normal developmental sequence; and

(c) the relative absence of concrete, abuse-focused treatment methodologies in the "self psychology" or "object relations" literatures (although see McCann & Pearlman, 1990). Fortunately, despite these difficulties it appears that extended, intensive psychotherapy can have significant and enduring impacts on the survivor's sense of, and access to, selfhood. The following are considerations and approaches that have proved helpful in addressing these abuse-related sequelae.

SAFETY AND SUPPORT
IN THE THERAPEUTIC RELATIONSHIP

Although support and caring are generic components of all good psychotherapy, individuals with difficulties in the self domain especially require a stable, positive environment in which to work. Hypervigilant survivors are unlikely to allow themselves the vulnerability inherent in growth and change if they can detect evidence of potential danger (e.g., via exploitation, disapproval, or rejection) in the therapeutic milieu. In some sense, consistent therapeutic safety reverses the dynamic referred to in Chapter 3 as "other-directedness." Whereas in childhood the victim was unable to develop full selfhood because he or she had to attend to chronic threats from others, a safe and supportive therapeutic relationship in adulthood frees the survivor to move attention from the external environment to internal experience. As the survivor explores this inner landscape, self-awareness and self-development can accrue.

Although the survivor may come to judge the immediate therapeutic context as benign, this is not equivalent to trusting the therapist. Instead, the more injured survivor is likely to experience brief periods of feeling safe enough to lessen his or her hypervigilance, only to move back into a defensive posture when disturbed by frightening internal or external stimuli. Ultimately, the client's perceptions of safety—prior to extended psychotherapy—may be understood as trust in his or her own ability to detect danger, as opposed to trust in the therapist not to be dangerous. As a result, the clinician must consistently demonstrate a caring, nonjudgmental, nonabusive demeanor, rather than assume at some point that the client's continuing sense of safety is a given.

THERAPIST FEEDBACK

As noted above, part of self work involves support for the survivor's growing acquaintance with internal states and events. With greater self-understanding, the survivor is more able to explore the logical basis for what previously may have appeared to be random or involuntary thoughts, affects, and behaviors. In this manner, the survivor slowly learns how to "own" his or her experience and behavior, with a resultant increase in self-determination and self-control.

In most cases, this process of self-exploration occurs in conjunction with specific types of therapist input. As therapy progresses, the clinician may offer the client feedback on her or his affect and behavior during the session, validate the client's fledgling positive self-perceptions, point out avoidant and/or dissociative responses, ask questions designed to stimulate self-exploration, or offer information on posttraumatic issues that may be relevant to the survivor's experience. The therapist may engage in what Kohut (1971) refers to as "positive mirroring," rephrasing negative client self-descriptions in more positive ways in order to encourage more benign self-perceptions (see the section on cognitive interventions later in this chapter for more on this approach).

It should be noted that all of these activities are designed to increase self-awareness or self-understanding, rather specifically stimulating self-development. Thus, for example, feedback to the client regarding feeling states or immediate behavior is intended to focus the survivor on what already exists "within" the client. This does not mean, however, that self-development does not occur during abuse-focused psychotherapy. As clients learn more about themselves, they more clearly understand their own needs and underlying motives, and so become better able to care for themselves without engaging in self-defeating or self-destructive behaviors. With improved self-nurturance, survivors develop greater self-confidence and self-support, resources that allow them to interact with the outside world in more complex ways and, as a result, develop more extensive repertoires of self-other behaviors. For many survivors, this growth process becomes most salient as they negotiate the therapeutic relationship and evolve through successively more complex and sophisticated roles with their therapists.

WORKING THROUGH DEPENDENCE
AND BOUNDARY CONFUSION
IN THE THERAPEUTIC RELATIONSHIP

Because the therapeutic relationship tends to elicit abuse-related needs, projections, and responses, it is not at all uncommon for dependency and boundary issues to arise during psychotherapy. The survivor may become extremely attached to the therapist, seemingly seeking the nurturance and support that was denied him or her early in life. Similarly, the client may experience boundary confusion as those self-other issues unresolved from childhood move to the forefront. Although these dynamics may be experienced as problematic by both survivor and therapist—for example, when they result in "primitive" client responses during treatment—this recapitulation of early childhood issues actually provides a major opportunity for survivor self-development. As she or he repetitively revisits early childhood experience in therapy, the client has the opportunity to rework early needs and perceptions in the context of a "new and improved" (nonabusive) other. In this way, the conundrum of "missed" stages of psychological development can be addressed in adulthood.

Much of the process of reworking childhood dependency and boundary issues involves the slow work of individuation from the therapist. In the context of the clinician's unconditional caring and support for self-awareness, the survivor becomes more and more able to react to interpersonal events without reflexive neediness or fear of separation. As a result, the survivor may begin to explore concerns and phenomena that previously were too far removed from basic survival to consider. Among other options, the client may experiment with autonomy—attempting behaviors that were too risky prior to consistent therapist support, such as standing up for him- or herself in conflicts with others or structuring the environment in ways that increase his or her mental or physical health. Eventually, as the survivor becomes more able to care for him- or herself, reliance on the therapist to provide this service wanes.

Similarly, the survivor's growing self-awareness and autonomy highlights differences between the client and the therapist, and reveals ways in which even the most benevolent of others cannot provide the survivor with some of the things the survivor him- or herself can.

Implicit in this process are at least two principles vis-à-vis therapist response to client dependence and boundary fusion. First, the survivor's dependence on the therapist is a healthy process, as opposed to one that should be discouraged or punished. Bowlby (1988), in fact, suggests that the word *dependence* should be replaced with *attachment* in such contexts, since the latter denotes the developmental basis for such behavior and avoids the negative implications of the former. The clinician is likely to be most helpful if he or she can provide appropriate levels of support during this attachment period, so that the client can evolve into a more autonomous position at his or her own pace. Therapists who prematurely push for client independence, ironically, may paradoxically reinforce dependency, as the survivor responds to perceived rejection with ever stronger clinging or "good client" behaviors. This does not mean, however, that the therapist should infantilize the client or demand or coerce dependency, or, in fact, that the clinician should gratify the client's every attachment need. Ultimately, the issue is how to nurture the survivor so that his or her therapy-appropriate needs can be met, and yet encourage the client's growth by providing opportunities for self-development.

A second principle is that of role-delineated caregiving. In his or her efforts to provide support and nurturance to the survivor, the therapist is subject to any unmet or unresolved needs to parent or, in fact, to join the client in the process of gratification. Thus implicit in therapeutic nurturance is role and boundary awareness. The effective therapist not only provides needed support and validation, but also communicates the importance of boundary appropriateness. As the client witnesses the therapist's unconditional caring as well as the therapist's unwillingness to move outside of the constraints of the therapeutic structure (e.g., to take the client home with him or her; to cuddle the client, in or out of sessions; or to allow phone calls to his or her home), a model for relationship delineation and respect is developed—a process that not only supports individuation, but also encourages the survivor to create different relationships to meet different needs.

SELF-SUPPORT TECHNIQUES

In addition to assisting with self-exploration and individuation, the abuse-focused therapist can bolster or increase self-relatedness by providing the survivor with self-support and self-nurturance techniques appropriate for use outside of the therapy session. Learned during therapy or via self-help books and tapes, these techniques provide the less self-referented survivor with needed props at times of crisis or extreme distress, as well as encouraging self-reliance and self-soothing. These activities can be divided into two general types: interruption of fragmenting processes and positive self-talk.

Interruption of Fragmenting Processes

As described by Bass and Davis (1986), Davis (1990), Gil (1983), Briere (1989) and others, there are a number of activities the survivor can engage in at times when crises or extreme affects have disrupted access to an integrated self, or have somehow reduced contact with external reality. "Grounding" (Blake-White & Kline, 1985), for example, is often used by survivors to lessen the extent or impacts of derealization or depersonalization, overwhelming rage or panic, repeated flashbacks, or intense reliving of traumatic events. The goal is to increase the survivor's sense of personal identity, contact with the here and now, and perceived personal control. Examples of grounding behaviors are repeating to oneself one's name, location, and immediate safety (e.g., "My name is Sarah, I'm at my cousin's house, I'm okay, I'm here, I'm real"), touching or concentrating on objects in the immediate environment, or feeling one's feet on the floor or one's body in a chair.

Another commonly used antifragmentation technique is that of distraction. The survivor may learn to turn to otherwise absorbing or engaging activities, such as reading, watching television, exercising, or conversing with others when confronted with escalating panic, repetitive flashbacks, or dissociative episodes. By diverting his or her attention away from these seemingly self-sustaining

internal events, the abuse survivor is often able to break the escala-
tion process long enough to regain cognitive control. For example,
the individual who is able to distract himself during an episode of
multiple flashbacks may discover that his nonattention to internal
events breaks the cycle of flashbacks restimulating new flashbacks
often associated with such episodes.

Finally, many survivors have discovered that the ability to self-
induce relaxation when necessary can be very helpful at times when
anxiety interferes with self-relatedness. Thus, for example, the abuse
survivor who has learned how to relax her body progressively and
slow her mental processes may be able to use this skill to terminate
or diminish episodes of self-fragmentation associated with acute
panic.

These and other activities may be learned during the course of
psychotherapy, typically when the client enters ego-dystonic states
of consciousness or experiences intrusive events. For example, the
client who vividly relives an instance of childhood rape during
treatment may be "brought back to reality" via therapist-assisted
grounding, relaxation, or distraction activities. As the survivor learns
how to engage in such activities by herself, she is increasingly able
to apply them to self-disrupting events that take place both within
and beyond the therapeutic environment.

Positive Self-Talk

In some ways similar to the self-statements found in grounding,
positive self-talk is a cognitive technique that has broad applications
for self-support. In contrast to the longer-term goals often addressed
by cognitive therapy (e.g., improved self-esteem or increased self-
efficacy), however, positive self-talk is more focused on acute concerns, such as increasing self-support during stress, countering
intrusive self-hatred, forestalling self-destructive activities, or reducing panic. For example, a survivor who finds herself losing track
of her needs or rights during an argument with her abusive spouse
might say things to herself such as, "He's wrong, I'm a good person,
and I don't deserve to be treated this way," or "Just because he says
that doesn't mean it's true." Similarly, a survivor about to engage in
self-destructive sexual behavior might remind himself, "I don't

have to do this to feel better—I can stop myself before I do something I'll regret later."

Positive self-talk is often first broached as an option when the client describes feelings of helplessness related to impaired self-reference. At such times, the clinician might ask the survivor, "How do you think you might help yourself when things like that happen? Is there anything that you could say to yourself that would calm you down/help you to stand up for yourself/stop you from hurting yourself at times like that?" Subsequently, the survivor may find it helpful to practice various self-supportive or self-soothing monologues, until he or she has a repertoire of positive self-descriptions available at times of diminished self-reference.

BUILDING AFFECT-REGULATION SKILLS

Abuse-related dissociation and tension-reduction activities used during childhood are thought to interfere with the development of later, more sophisticated, self functions, especially those involving affect modulation skills. Affects most likely to be dissociated or avoided seem to be those most dangerous or unacceptable during the survivor's childhood, such as anger, or those whose complete experience would have overwhelmed the survivor's early affect-regulation system, such as terror. The short-term effectiveness of dissociation and tension reduction also appears to lessen the survivor's need to develop sustained tolerance for such painful internal states. Unfortunately, dissociation and tension-reduction behaviors are, almost by definition, primitive—responses that tend to operate in a relative "all-or-nothing" manner rather than on a continuum that can be modulated according to the type and extent of internal distress. Further, dissociation and primitive tension-reduction activities can be maladaptive or injurious by virtue of their inherent properties (e.g., drug abuse or indiscriminate sex) or because of their tendency to reduce the survivor's accurate responsiveness to environmental demands.

As indicated in Chapter 5, an integral part of abuse-focused therapy is the client's self-exposure to manageable quantities of abuse-related distress. The therapist must monitor this process carefully; insufficient processing of traumatic experience will accomplish little, whereas too much exposure may flood the survivor with painful affect. Although a major goal of controlled access to trauma is the desensitization and integration of painful states and memories, as discussed later in this chapter, this process also stimulates the development of affect-regulation skills.

By encouraging the survivor to confront and process manageable abuse-related affects while at the same time discouraging the overuse of affect avoidance techniques such as dissociation, abuse-focused therapy allows the survivor to experiment with more sophisticated approaches to affect modulation—responses that could not be learned during the terror and overwhelming pain of childhood abuse. Further, carefully titrated exposure to abuse trauma can provide the survivor with opportunities to learn how to tolerate tolerable pain, rather than reflexively turning to dissociation or tension reduction. Thus therapeutic approaches introduced in Chapter 5, such as balancing exploration with consolidation, intensity control, and differential time focus, are used by the clinician to provide a "window" of optimally challenging affective experience, wherein the survivor can develop improved emotional regulation without sacrificing safety or control.

Affect-regulation skills are often developed during the therapeutic processing of (a) abuse-related material and (b) issues restimulated during transference. In the former case, controlled emotional processing of abuse memories—at whatever level the survivor can tolerate—provides an environment where the survivor can experiment with safe and nonoverwhelming levels of anger, sorrow, or fear. As a result, the survivor develops a slowly growing capacity to feel "at home" with such affects, rather than immediately expelling them from awareness via dissociation or tension reduction. This process eventually results in decreased psychological "symptoms," since the survivor less frequently needs to turn to activities such as substance abuse, self-mutilation, or dissociative states to modulate abuse-restimulated affects.

The exploration of transferential issues and responses, especially when both thoughts and affects are addressed in therapy, offers many opportunities to learn adaptive affect regulation. The survivor's projection of early perceptions and experiences onto the therapist is typically accompanied by emotional responses to those projections, as well as by restimulated abuse-era affects. As a result, the client is likely to experience feelings that were unacceptable or dangerous during his or her childhood abuse, but that are now possible to express in the safety of the therapy session. For example, the child whose natural anger at her abuser had to be dissociated or sublimated through tension reduction for safety reasons, or who was rejected or ignored by her parents whenever she was angry, may continue to have problems tolerating or modulating anger later in life. In therapy, her repeated projections of angry feelings onto the clinician—who does not punish or reject her for such affects, but may find it necessary to set limits on her angry behavior—allows the survivor to become more familiar with the feeling and expression of anger. This increasing familiarity, in turn, supports the survivor's growing ability to tolerate and negotiate angry affect when it occurs.

The reader will note the extensive overlap between therapeutic approaches to affect regulation and, as described later in this chapter, the treatment of posttraumatic stress. The primary differences between these two domains are of therapeutic goal and timing: The intent of affect-regulation interventions is to improve the survivor's ability to experience and tolerate abuse-related distress and dysphoria, whereas more classical "trauma work" builds on this capacity in order to desensitize and integrate the trauma that initially produced such affects. As noted in Chapter 5, the latter is predicated on reasonable success at the former.

❏ Cognitive Interventions

Aaron

As presented in the section on cognitive distortions in Chapter 2, Aaron is in therapy to address the effects of extensive psychological maltreatment he received as a child. Much of his therapist's time is devoted to gentle, respectful disagreements with Aaron regarding his value as a human being, the extent of his self-efficacy, and his rights in relationships with others. Such are his self-esteem problems that even positive statements from others are seen as evidence that he is a bad person—data that he is so disturbed as to be unable to see his own positive qualities. Nevertheless, his therapist's patient and steadfast reframing of his negative self-evaluations and normalization of his daily experience are beginning to pay off: Aaron appears to be more able to see his cognitive distortions as such, rather than as accurate negative perceptions of himself and the world around him. In Aaron's case, the combination of cognitive therapy techniques presented below and those "self"-focused interventions described previously work especially well together, offering him the fledgling possibility that his capacities, options, and prospects far exceed what he was taught to accept as a child.

As noted in Chapters 2 and 3, child abuse almost inevitably distorts perceptions of self, other people, the future, and the world. As a result, many survivors are prone to some combination of guilt, low self-esteem, pessimism, and fearful expectations of the interpersonal environment. These sequelae are well known to cognitive therapists, who have developed specific interventions to address "erroneous" thoughts and assumptions (see, e.g., Beck, 1976; Beck & Emery, 1985; Ellis, 1977; Meichenbaum, 1977). Although the reader is referred to this literature for detailed information on the theory and techniques of cognitive therapy, certain aspects of abuse-focused treatment explicitly involve cognitive interventions, and are outlined below.

THE COGNITIVE APPROACH TO ABUSE TRAUMA

From a cognitive perspective, effective psychotherapy of abuse trauma must include interventions that help the survivor to update his or her victimization-related assumptions. The client is taught to recognize and alter abuse-distorted thoughts, beliefs, and perceptions through what is referred to as *cognitive restructuring*. As noted by Jehu (1988), such activities help survivors "a) to become aware of their beliefs; b) to recognize any distortions they contain; and c) to substitute more accurate alternative beliefs" (p. 57).

The survivor is encouraged to examine the objective and historic bases for his or her most painful abuse-related assumptions. For example, Jehu (1988) suggests addressing beliefs such as "I am worthless and bad," "I must have been seductive and provocative when I was young," and "I am inferior to other people because I did not have normal experiences" (p. 319). In each of these instances, a cognitive approach might lead to therapist responses such as "I wonder where you learned to see yourself like that?" "What about being abused makes you inferior?" and "Last week we talked about how scared and helpless you felt as a child—how does that fit with what you're saying now about being seductive?" Thus the therapist offers gentle challenges to the survivor's abuse-distorted view of him- or herself and others, so that the survivor may begin to construct a worldview less influenced by childhood oppression.

Normalization

Normalization refers to cognitive interventions that help the survivor to understand the abuser's (as opposed to the survivor's) responsibility for child abuse and that identify the logical ("normal") basis for the survivor's postvictimization reactions. In each case, the clinician attempts to alter the client's abuse-related self-perceptions of stigma, abnormality, or malignancy. As noted above, many abuse survivors believe that they in some way caused their abuse by deserving it, precipitating it, or not stopping it from happening. Similarly, adults abused as children often view their current responses or adaptations to childhood victimization as further evidence of badness, inadequacy, or mental disorder. As cognitive theorists have noted in more general contexts, such attributions or assumptions frequently lead to negative mood states (e.g., depression or anxiety) or altered behavior patterns (e.g., self-destructive activities, impaired self-assertion, or avoidance of the social milieu).

Perhaps the most common form of normalization is communication to the survivor that the abuse was neither deserved nor the survivor's fault, and that he or she is not currently a bad or defective person as a result of such victimization. This process may be accomplished by (a) the clinician's ongoing, gentle rejection of client self-derogation and self-blame, (b) consistent therapeutic reframing of abuse-related "symptoms" as adaptive or logical responses, and (c) introduction of the client to books or other media that describe the commonness and diverse impacts of child abuse, affirm the struggles of abuse survivors, and stress the perpetrator's or society's responsibility for child victimization. By virtue of their unambiguous rejection of survivor badness or deservingness of victimization, such activities may be distinguished from more passive or "objective" therapies that rely on eventual client inferences regarding self-value or childhood responsibility.

Intervention in Self-Derogation

Therapist response to client self-derogation should balance confrontation of inaccurate self-perceptions with the need, in effect, to avoid blaming the client for self-blame. Badly done cognitive therapy may subtly reinforce low self-esteem with contradictory statements such as "There you go again, putting yourself down," or "Why do you always have to end every sentence with something bad about yourself?" Because the survivor is often primed to expect negative evaluation and abusive treatment from authority figures, the clinician must be especially careful to phrase feedback in a supportive and nonblaming manner. Thus the therapist might use statements such as "It sounds like when you talk about _____ you automatically think negative thoughts about yourself. Why do you think that is?" or "Did you notice how you described yourself when you talked about your dad? What do you think that's about?" Ultimately, the intent is to communicate nonagreement with client self-derogation while simultaneously supporting the notion of a shared client-therapist agenda: jointly to undo abuse effects by calling attention to automatic self-devaluating assumptions, as opposed to correcting the survivor's inherent personal failings.

Because client self-criticism is often so pervasive, there may be a tendency for the therapist to overlook some self-negating comments. While understandable, this action can inadvertently reinforce the survivor's low self-regard. The client whose statement "Not that I deserve it, but I still think she could have been nicer to me" goes uncontested, for example, may assume that the therapist's nonresponse reveals a secret belief in the client's undeservingness. For this reason, it is recommended that the clinician always "go on the record" when the client expresses self-derogation or self-devaluation. Such responses need not be stale repetitions about the client's value or tendency toward self-criticism; the creative therapist is usually able to find a variety of ways to communicate gentle, authentic disagreement with negative client self-perceptions.

Reframing of "Symptoms"

An important cognitive component of abuse-focused therapy is the explicit reanalysis of "pathological" or "symptomatic" behaviors as, instead, logical extensions of early responses to child abuse. The notion that abuse-related behavior is not reflective of illness potentially increases the survivor's sense of self-control (as opposed to control by a disease process), and removes the stigma inherent in being defined in terms of pathology. Sadly, clinicians who adhere to a medical model when working with abuse survivors can do the reverse: By referring to "symptoms" and "disorders" when describing abuse sequelae, they can further complicate or intensify client stigmatization.

As noted in Chapter 2, abuse-related "symptomatic" behaviors often reflect functional responses—ways in which the survivor adapted to a violent or chaotic environment. Frequent communication of this fact to the survivor is often helpful in increasing the survivor's willingness to trust him- or herself as a caretaker, as well as decreasing his or her sense of inherent badness. If, in fact, the survivor has not been sick, but instead has been adapting and surviving, the focus ceases to be on "dysfunctional behavior" or inherent self-destructiveness. Instead, the issue becomes one of surviving better, of developing even more effective strategies for living. To the extent that the survivor is able to adopt this perspective, he or she is less likely to feel helpless or deficient.

In practice, therapeutic reframing of "symptomatology" involves both provision of information on the adaptive and pragmatic aspects of various survivor behaviors and intervention in client statements that reflect pathologizing self-perspectives. For example, the clinician might suggest that self-mutilation or binging reflects attempts by the survivor to reduce painful abuse-related states, or that the survivor's "seductive" behavior represents instrumental activity designed to ensure physical nurturance or increased self-esteem.

Further, the clinician might gently disagree with the survivor that flashbacks are signs of being crazy, and instead might suggest that such experiences represent the mind's attempt to heal itself by reexposing the survivor to small, "handle-able" chunks of painful memory.

It should be noted that reframing seemingly pathological responses or behaviors does not always mean supporting the use of these activities in the future. For example, although self-mutilation, indiscriminate sex, and substance abuse might be explainable as logical survival behaviors, the clinician will ideally work with the survivor to develop less injurious, more self-affirming, ways to deal with painful states or experiences. Thus the critical notion is the destigmatization of the survivor's experience through contextualization of his or her behavior, as opposed to unquestioning reinforcement of the behavior in question.

Use of Books and Other Media

As noted earlier in this chapter, a recent development in the abuse field has been the availability of books and tapes created explicitly for the survivor, especially those who have experienced sexual abuse. These materials are often quite helpful for former child abuse victims, both in and out of therapy. Most noteworthy is their focus: They usually discuss the elevated incidence and social context of child abuse, outline typical effects of abuse in a nonpathologizing manner, and, perhaps most important, offer the survivor concrete assistance with abuse-related problems and intrusive abuse-related states. Bass and Davis's (1986) *The Courage to Heal,* for example, includes sections on ways the survivor can terminate painful flashbacks, reduce dissociative states, address substance abuse, and avoid acting on suicidal thoughts. Similarly, Gil's (1983) *Outgrowing the Pain* provides an easily understood description of abuse-related difficulties and offers concrete advice regarding their resolution, whereas Lew's (1990) *Victims No Longer* is especially helpful in normalizing the experience of male sexual abuse survivors. Finally, Maltz's (1991) *The Sexual Healing Journey* provides extensive information, suggestions, and exercises for the sexual difficulties that many survivors experience. By the time this book goes to press, a number of additional books for survivors undoubtedly will be available.

Also available are a number of films and tapes, including, for example, the excellent *Healing Sexual Abuse: The Recovery Process*, hosted by Eliana Gil and produced by KCET Video in Los Angeles, California. As is also true of the books noted above, the clinician should personally review any videos or audiotapes before suggesting them to clients, because such media can be variable in their content and quality.

Although these various resources were developed primarily as self-help materials, they can serve as powerful adjuncts to ongoing psychotherapy. For example, relevant chapters in self-help books can be read as homework during treatment, either to reinforce insights developed during a given session or to provide more in-depth information on a specific issue than can reasonably be addressed during therapy. There may be an additional benefit for some survivors: Independent verification of the therapist's reframings or suggestions by an outside source may increase the likelihood that they will be accepted by the client. In a tangential example of this phenomenon, one 27-year-old client in abuse-focused therapy was able to consider her blamelessness for her molestation only after hearing similar statements made by others on Oprah Winfrey's television show.

Although many self-help books and tapes are quite effective in addressing abuse-related cognitive sequelae, others may be less helpful. Volumes that overemphasize addictions, personal responsibility for one's past, or the importance of "positive thinking" as opposed to working through abuse-related pain, for example, may impede the work of psychotherapy. It is obviously not appropriate for the therapist to forbid or even unduly discourage the reading of such books. In such instances, however, he or she may choose to suggest additional books more relevant to abuse-focused therapy and hope for the best.

As may be apparent from this section, many aspects of abuse-focused psychotherapy are inherently cognitive in nature. To the extent that the therapist explains, teaches, suggests, or gently confronts the survivor, he or she is doing cognitive therapy. To the extent that this process honors the dignity and value of the client, it is especially likely to be helpful for abuse survivors.

❑ Exploration and Desensitization of Trauma

Alicia

Alicia was 17 years old when she presented to a psychiatric emergency room with significant posttraumatic stress, apparently the result of severe sexual, physical, and emotional abuse during childhood. Now in her early 20s, she is completing her second year of treatment with a psychiatric resident specializing in psychological trauma. Initially, when recounting sexual violence in her childhood, Alicia would become quite agitated and dissociated, often to the point where no further work could be done in that session. As treatment has progressed, however, and after many hours of struggling to describe and reexperience every traumatic incident she could recall, these memories no longer have such anxiety-eliciting effects, nor do they motivate obvious dissociation or other defensive responses. She has since recovered other, even more violent, memories, and has processed these in treatment as well. A more general result of therapy is that Alicia seems to be less fearful of strong affect per se and is considerably more effective in dealing with feelings of anxiety, sadness, and anger when they occur.

As described in Chapter 2, many people who were physically or sexually abused as children experience signs of posttraumatic stress later in life, including flashbacks, nightmares, dissociation, and fearful avoidance. These difficulties are referred to as *posttraumatic* because they are thought to arise from discrete, especially upsetting events, as opposed to, for example, the more chronic and insidious stressors inherent in psychological maltreatment or emotional neglect. According to McCann and Pearlman (1990):

An experience is traumatic if it (1) is sudden, unexpected, or non-normative, (2) exceeds the individual's perceived ability to meet its demands, and (3) disrupts the individual's frame of reference and other central psychological needs and related schemas. The first part of the definition serves to exclude the chronic difficulties of life, which, although themselves important and at times severe, must be distinguished from trauma if the construct is to serve any heuristic purpose. (p. 10)

Although I view trauma more broadly (hence, for example, the title of this book), McCann and Pearlman's definition describes well the kinds of events required to produce flashbacks, especially intrusive memories, and other signs of post-traumatic stress disorder. Such problems are well known to specialists in psychological trauma, who have developed techniques and perspectives especially relevant to work with victims of war, natural disasters, human-made catastrophes, and—most recently—former victims of sexual and physical child abuse.

The application of trauma theory to abuse survivors, primarily by writers such as Gelinas (1983), Herman and van der Kolk (1987), McCann and Pearlman (1990), and Meiselman (1990), focuses therapeutic attention on the defensive and adaptive components of postabuse sequelae. From this perspective, severe sexual and/or physical abuse is seen as a stressor that would induce significant psychological disturbance in almost anyone, such that later "abnormal" behavior is reinterpreted as situationally appropriate coping responses and/or normal reactions to an overwhelmingly aversive event.

As clinicians in this area suggest, memories of severe childhood victimization are often at least partially repressed, avoided, compartmentalized, or otherwise dissociated from awareness in order to reduce painful abuse-related affect. Trauma-based interventions therefore tend to focus on two tasks:

1. the recovery and exploration of previously avoided or repressed memories of childhood maltreatment
2. the working through and desensitization of painful affects (i.e., anxiety, depression, rage) associated with new abuse-related awareness

The goal is the integration of split-off cognitions, affects, and memories into conscious awareness, so that there is less need for dissociation or tension-reducing behaviors to control abuse-related distress.

EXPLORATION OF MEMORIES

Available Memories

Although trauma specialists often stress the importance of work with repressed or incomplete memories, abuse-focused psychotherapy even more commonly addresses memories that are already present at the time of treatment. Exploration of these memories serves several goals:

1. The therapist obtains data on the characteristics of the abuse, as well as the survivor's current and historic responses to them.
2. The client has the opportunity to consider her or his victimization in detail, thereby potentially lessening the power of denial and other defenses to minimize the abuse and its impacts.
3. Emotional catharsis (described below) may occur as affects associated with traumatic memory are restimulated and reexperienced without major dissociation.
4. Previously repressed material may emerge as conscious memory is expanded.
5. The recounting of childhood memories out loud and in front of another person may allow the survivor to update her or his perceptions and reactions to the abuse, rather than viewing them as she or he did during childhood.
6. Painful affects associated with the recall of abuse events can be reduced or eliminated through the repetitive exploration of these memories in a safe environment.

Even though conscious memories of childhood trauma are technically available to the abuse survivor, she or he may attempt to suppress or withhold them during treatment. Among the motives for inhibiting the disclosure and exploration of abuse memories are avoidance of dysphoria (e.g., anxiety, disgust, humiliation, or embarrassment), fear of being overwhelmed or losing control, expectations of negative judgment, and the desire to minimize one's history by leaving it unspoken. Such concerns make it nearly impossible for the clinician to be a passive, detached receiver of survivor memories. Instead, the therapist must actively work to convey safety, a willingness to believe what is expressed, and a level of supportiveness that extends beyond mere nonjudgment.

By virtue of his or her visible acceptance of painful information without disgust, shock, or pity, the effective clinician also communicates competence as a facilitator. This message of stability and understanding encourages the client to delegate to the therapist at least briefly some aspects of his or her safety and survival. The clinician, in turn, must be prepared to take this responsibility seriously, by, for example, providing ongoing reassurance, validating the survivor's early and current responses, avoiding stigmatizing interpretations, and structuring the interaction so that the survivor is neither overwhelmed by extreme affect nor left with excessive arousal at session's end.

Assuming the client is at some point able to recount some of his or her childhood victimization experiences, the clinician's next task is to ensure adequate exploration of these memories. As presented by McCann and Pearlman (1990), this requires attention to both "verbal" and "imagery" systems of memory. Because these authors so aptly describe this principle, the reader is referred to the chapter "Resolving Traumatic Memories" in their book *Psychological Trauma and the Adult Survivor*. In brief, however, McCann and Pearlman (1990, p. 205) recommend the clinician access verbal aspects of traumatic memories by asking questions such as the following:

- What is the first thing you remember about what happened?
- What happened next?
- What is the last thing you remember happening?
- Can you clearly remember the sequence of events or the time frame?

Imagery components of the memory, on the other hand, are explored with questions such as these:

- When you remember what happened, do you see any pictures in your mind?
- Can you see colors?
- Can you see what you were wearing?
- Are you aware of any smells, sounds, bodily sensations?

Many survivors are more able to provide verbal-analytic renditions of their abuse than they are the associated sensory components. By including the latter domain, the clinician may facilitate a more integrated (less dissociated) reexperiencing of abusive events, and thus potentially a more complete resolution of posttraumatic difficulties. Some clinicians, in fact, encourage clients to draw, paint, or in some other nonverbal modality depict their abuse experiences in order to access the less linear, more sensory components of abuse-specific memory (see, e.g., Courtois, 1988; Greenberg & van der Kolk, 1987).

Repressed or Dissociated Memories

As noted earlier, it appears that severe postabuse trauma may be associated with at least partial amnesia for abuse-related phenomena. Studies by Briere and Conte (in press) and Herman and Schatzow (1987), for example, indicate that complete or partial amnesia for abuse events was present in more than half of two samples of clinical sexual abuse survivors, and that those abuse episodes most likely to be repressed were ones involving earlier, more violent victimization. This process appears to reflect the active, but unconscious, decision of the survivor to inhibit recall of events that would produce extreme distress if acknowledged. I have described this previously as a variant of what Hilgard (1986) calls the "hidden observer" in hypnosis: an aspect of personality unaffected by dissociative processes that determines how much "reality" the survivor can tolerate, and titrates awareness or recall accordingly (Briere, 1989). Meiselman (1990) posits a similar process with regard to amnesia, which she refers to as the incest survivor's "internal wisdom" (p. 144).

The relevance of such unconscious decision making to treatment is that amnesia becomes less a pathological process and more an adaptive strategy. As a result, the clinician should carefully consider the validity of methods that dramatically increase access to repressed memories, since the unconscious communication from the survivor (by virtue of the amnesia) is that he or she does not believe complete knowledge is in his or her immediate best interests. The psychotherapist who overlooks this communication runs the risk of moving too fast: exposing the survivor to information and experiences that may exceed his or her internal resources and affect regulation capacity, thereby precipitating a crisis and/or involvement in repetitive tension-reduction activities.

There appear to be instances, however, when abuse-related memory deficits do not arise from unconscious decisions to be unaware. Research on "state-dependent learning" suggests that some difficulties in postabuse recall may result from the fact that experiences stored in memory under extreme arousal conditions may not be retrievable except during equivalent psychological states (van der Kolk, 1989). Thus the survivor whose abuse occurred under conditions of extreme fear or shock (for example, during a violent rape or a potentially deadly assault) may not have access to such memories when in a more "normal" (lower or different) arousal state; for instance, during the typical psychotherapy session. Such recall may be further complicated by what can be described as *dissociative inattention*: the impacts of abuse-concurrent dissociation on memory acquisition during victimization. One might expect, for example, that the victim who attenuates sensory input during violent abuse to avoid overwhelming pain and psychological trauma would be more likely to "miss" aspects of his or her abuse than would someone who had less need to call on extreme dissociative defenses.

Although recall under the inattention condition may be virtually impossible to obtain, techniques that allow the survivor to "return" to the original abuse event (e.g., through guided imagery) may replicate enough of the survivor's original affective experience to allow recovery of state-dependent material. Caution is obviously indicated here, however, since those procedures most effective in recreating the abuse scenario run the risk of retraumatizing the client through reexposure to memory of highly aversive events that he or she is not prepared for. As a result, most clinicians who use hypnosis or guided imagery for this purpose stress the need to limit the maximum amount of distress the survivor can undergo, and usually build into the hypnotic induction some sort of automatic defense the survivor can utilize (see, for example, Dolan, 1991; Spiegel, 1989).

Another way in which the survivor may reenter abuse-similar affective experience is through gradually more detailed exploration of abuse memories during regular psychotherapy. For example, as

the client recalls a small fragment of a traumatic experience, associated thoughts, memories, feelings, and transferential reactions are
often evoked, thereby leading further into the memory. As a result,
the survivor is able slowly to re-create abuse-related affective and
cognitive experience, often allowing further access to state-dependent material. This process has advantages over hypnosis in that it
(a) arises smoothly and in an integrated fashion from the process of
treatment, rather than switching to a new therapeutic modality, and
(b) unfolds more clearly under the client's control, at his or her own
pace.

Most basically, memory exploration that does not rely on special
techniques (e.g., hypnosis) calls instead upon the safety, trust, and
connectedness of the positive therapeutic relationship (Courtois, in
press; Gil, 1988). In many cases, in fact, a reciprocal process emerges: Therapeutic safety and support encourage memory recall, and
growing recall reinforces the validity and importance of the therapeutic relationship. As noted by Meiselman (1990):

> The slow and careful building of trust in the therapeutic relationship
> has been strongly emphasized because it is the safest method for facil-
> itating derepression and consequent reintegration. This trust building
> is the therapist's major task, and the use of any specific technique to
> break through repression is questionable. . . . these techniques [e.g.,
> hypnosis] should not be viewed as shortcuts that can provide a quick
> and easy solution to the incest survivor's problem. (pp. 143-144)

Given the importance of honoring the survivor's unconscious
wishes regarding abuse-related awareness, as well as the potential
impacts of state dependence on recall, the relative importance of
complete memory recovery in the treatment of postabuse trauma is
a subject of controversy among clinicians. Although some therapists
appear to suggest that most or all major abuse-relevant memories
must be accessed and worked through before trauma can be resolved, others (myself included) are less convinced of this. It is
likely, in fact, that many clients will never recover all—or even most
—memories of traumatic childhood experience. Fortunately, effective trauma-focused treatment often appears to have a generic impact on relationship to painful memory, such that working through
available (or eventually available) memories decreases the power of

unavailable material to produce dysphoria or motivate tension reduction. It is my experience, for example, that as important memories are addressed and desensitized in therapy, the client gains skill in dealing with painful recall per se. As a result, memories that emerge later in life (or considerably later in therapy) may not produce the level of stress or distress that was present when early abuse-relevant memories were accessed. Exceptions to this tendency do occur, of course, including instances where later memories are so traumatic (e.g., of ritualistic abuse or especially humiliating or guilt-producing events) that the survivor enters or reenters a posttraumatic crisis upon recall.

Unfortunately, a number of clients and therapists appear driven to expose and confront every possible traumatic memory potentially associated with a given instance of child abuse. When this occurs for survivors, there may be insistent requests for hypnosis, Pentothal interviews, or other special interventions that will "help me remember." If memory recovery is especially the therapist's issue, there may be extended and intense efforts to somehow make the client uncover all traumatic material—often to the detriment of other therapeutic tasks, such as support, consolidation, desensitization, or emotional insight. As suggested earlier, the process of memory recovery should be a gentle, nonintrusive one—a process that respects the survivor's unconscious choice not to remember certain things at certain times, sometimes despite his or her conscious statements.

EMOTIONAL PROCESSING

As important as access to memories of childhood trauma is, such activity is unlikely to be especially helpful in the absence of concomitant emotional experience and expression. The survivor whose recall of seemingly painful material occurs solely in an intellectual mode is usually utilizing dissociation, a mechanism that prevents simultaneous cognitive and emotional processing and thus can impede a complete working through of the trauma. Abuse-focused therapy instead seeks to foster the client's healthy (nondissociated) experience of the strong feelings connected with trauma-specific memory—sometimes referred to as *catharsis* or, if the memory had previously been repressed, *abreaction*.

Adequate catharsis of previously dissociated trauma seems to complete an emotional gestalt; the human organism may require repeated emotional discharge, without significant dissociation, in order to recover completely from traumatic experiences. Ross (1989), for example, notes that "intense reliving of abuse in the presence of a therapist seems to be part of getting better, much like inflammation is part of the natural healing process" (p. 248). Repeated emotional processing of traumatic memories during therapy can also increase the client's affective tolerance—teaching him or her how to experience the intense feelings associated with upsetting events and restimulated trauma without becoming overwhelmed or prematurely resorting to tension-reduction behaviors.

For these reasons, abuse-focused therapy is likely to be more emotionally involving for the survivor than, for example, purely cognitive or traditional psychodynamic approaches. A considerable portion of the therapist's time is devoted to supporting emotional expression, whether it be the survivor's response to current life events or the ventilation of affects associated with memories of childhood injury. In order to maximize this process, most trauma-focused clinicians engage in at least three different tasks: facilitating emotional discharge, gently interfering with reflexive dissociation, and normalizing strong affect.

Some clinicians may find the goal of facilitating emotional release somewhat alien, especially if their approach to treatment is usually more cognitive. This work is nevertheless necessary, since many abuse survivors have difficulty with the experience and expression of painful affect. Even the "histrionic" survivor, in fact, may be uncomfortable with strong feelings, instead defensively engaging in "as if" dissociation (Briere, 1989)—assuming the role of someone who is having the feelings that the survivor, in fact, needs to have. In either instance, whether during affective avoidance or "as if" emotionality, the survivor can benefit from therapeutic interventions that allow integrated ventilation of affect without reflexive dissociation or perceived loss of control. The value of such emotional discharge has been documented for combat veterans, rape victims, and others who have been psychologically traumatized

(Burgess & Holmstrom, 1979; Kolb, 1984; van der Kolk, 1987), as well as for abuse victims and survivors (Briere, 1989; Courtois, 1988; Meiselman, 1990).

Although many survivors have compartmentalized, distanced, or otherwise attenuated painful abuse-related feelings, abuse therapists often find that such individuals have strong affect just beneath the surface, emotions that can be accessed in the presence of empathic, caring, gently exploratory therapist responses. This may be due, in part, to the potential for psychotherapy to restimulate abuse-related issues, as well as its support for reduced defensiveness and thus greater emotional vulnerability. Ultimately, however, this easily triggered emotionality appears to reflect both the pain inherent in abuse trauma and the brittleness of most survivors' defenses against such pain.

Although survivor anxiety, rage, or sadness can be elicited directly in some instances, the client is often unable and/or unwilling to remain in such painful states for long. Instead, she or he may marshal any number of dissociative defenses, including detachment, derealization, numbing, or intellectualization. The clinician can intervene in such activities by, for example, asking the survivor to identify and describe immediate feelings, encouraging him or her to "stay with" emotional experience, or commenting on the presence of specific dissociative behaviors during treatment (for other interventions helpful in dealing with therapy-specific dissociation, see Briere, 1989). The goal of this process is that of affective tolerance, as described earlier in this chapter—to increase the survivor's ability to experience painful affect for longer periods of time without significant dissociation or tension-reduction behaviors and to help the survivor discover that, in fact, strong feelings are merely feelings, not harbingers of impending annihilation or dangerous loss of control.

To the extent that the survivor can sustain an abuse-relevant feeling state, he or she will benefit from immediate therapeutic validation of the experience. The clinician usually stresses the normality of having strong feelings or of engaging in emotional catharsis, and decatastrophizes the client's fearful cognitions. The clinician may repeatedly indicate that the client is not going crazy, losing control, or humiliating him- or herself by virtue of less inhibited emotional expression, but instead is experiencing a natural, restorative process. Normalization of emotional discharge must be conveyed in more than words, however. The clinician who verbally validates extreme anger or anguish but at the same time withdraws or appears shocked, for example, is likely to communicate a common social message: that some emotions are worse than others, and that giving in to the full expression of certain feelings is a sign of badness, weakness, or psychopathology.

In order to be maximally helpful, therapists must come to terms not only with their own issues related to strong emotion per se, but also with the inevitability of "negative" affect in their clients. They must reconcile themselves to an essential aspect of trauma: It is usually the most painful and unacceptable of things that motivate sustained emotional avoidance. Because of their dissociated, ego-dystonic qualities, formerly suppressed or repressed feelings are often quite extreme and, to some extent, socially unacceptable when completely expressed. Given social and personal avoidance of intense affects such as rage, despair, terror, and revulsion, clinicians must be all the more prepared to validate and support these abuse-appropriate responses when they emerge during treatment.

Process Desensitization

In addition to altering the client's response to (and processing of) abuse-related affect, interventions that address posttraumatic emotionality tend to reduce the negative valence of painful recollections. This occurs when memories of traumatic events are repeatedly evoked and explored in a safe, nonpainful environment. Referred to here as *process desensitization*, this aspect of posttraumatic therapy breaks the previously conditioned association between traumatic memory and anxiety or revulsion by, instead, pairing such memories with contemporary therapeutic support and the relief associated with safe emotional discharge. As a result, the client slowly becomes emotionally desensitized to abuse-related memories and is more able to discuss, explore, and integrate them into awareness without resorting to distress-reducing defenses that interfere with adequate emotional processing.

The unlinking of previously traumatic memories and acute distress typically occurs in a stepwise manner: As one abuse memory is gradually desensitized and integrated, there is often sufficient de-arousal that the need for dissociation decreases and another memory can move to the forefront and, in turn, be desensitized and integrated. Over time, this working through of one abuse memory after another results in the survivor's growing ability to address past experiences in a flexible, nonfearful manner, and thereby gain greater mastery over such recollections. Furthermore, the reduced tendency for memories to stimulate anxiety decreases the survivor's need to engage in tension-reducing behaviors (i.e., "symptoms") when exposed to abuse-related stimuli or thoughts.

Finally, process desensitization of abuse trauma operates on a more global level. A caring, supportive therapeutic environment in which the client is valued unconditionally is likely to reduce abuse-related anxiety regarding close, psychologically intimate relationships. In the optimal situation, the client may come to associate at least one relationship with safety and positivity, rather than with danger, intrusion, or adversariality. Over time, this learning may generalize to other settings, leading to greater trust (when indicated) and improved self-efficacy in various social domains.

WORK IN ABSENTIA

A final component of abuse-focused therapy is the use of therapeutic activities outside of the psychotherapy session. Most commonly this involves writing in a journal on a regular basis or completing exercises in specially designed self-help books (such as Davis's *The Courage to Heal Workbook*, 1990). The benefits of such activities are manifold:

1. They reinforce self-support (many survivors, for example, report writing at length when upset or confused, until they become calm or reach some sort of resolution).
2. They provide an opportunity for the survivor to work directly on abuse issues outside of the therapy session.
3. They help the survivor to access her or his creativity, thereby bringing a positive force into the growth process.

4. They chronicle the survivor's experience and growth over time, thereby providing a sense of continuity and perspective.
5. They offer a partial solution to the state dependence described earlier in this chapter.

With regard to the last point, many survivors find it helpful to bring into the therapy session material they wrote during an earlier dissociated and/or highly dysphoric period. For example, a client who has intermittent episodes of autistic withdrawal, self-mutilatory urges, and intrusive flashbacks at 3:00 a.m., but who is unable to communicate those feelings and experiences the next day due to state dependence, may be able to enter and describe that state at least partially when reading her journal entry to her therapist. As a result, the therapist has access to information unlikely to be available in the average therapy session, and the survivor has the opportunity to address experiences and responses that otherwise would not be evident during treatment. In the extreme case, there have been instances when both survivor and therapist have reviewed material that suggests the previously unidentified presence of severely split-off ego states or of a multiple personality disorder (e.g., different writing styles or obviously different developmental levels).

❏ Summary

This chapter has described a variety of techniques and approaches that have proved helpful in the treatment of postabuse trauma. The diversity of these interventions attests to the complexity and pervasiveness of child abuse sequelae, and reinforces the need for an eclectic, multimodal approach to the treatment of adults abused as children. As noted earlier, however, any or all of these techniques will be useful only to the extent that the clinician actively conveys respect, acceptance, and validation during the psychotherapy process, and stays attuned to the client's needs for safety and control over the optimal level of therapeutic intensity.

7

Special Issues in Abuse-Focused Therapy

Although the previous chapters have outlined some essentials of abuse-focused psychotherapy, there are a number of additional issues that can arise during the treatment of adults abused as children. This final chapter briefly addresses some of those questions most often asked during workshops and lectures on abuse-specific therapy. Many represent concerns that remain open questions because we have not yet advanced sufficiently as a field to have definitive answers in all areas. Thus, although I attempt to offer schematic advice wherever possible, each of these questions represents a topic for further clinical and research exploration.

❏ Treatment-Based
Exacerbation of Symptoms

Alanna

As described in Chapter 1, Alanna is in treatment to address her problems with substance abuse, self-mutilation, and a variety of interpersonal difficulties related to having been raped by her father and brother from ages 7 to 16. As therapy proceeds, Alanna has recovered new memories of violent victimization, and has become increasingly preoccupied with fears of abandonment by her male psychiatrist. Although she and her therapist believe she is progressing in therapy, she is becoming more and more depressed and anxious, and has gone on several cocaine binges of late—on each occasion of which she has cut on her arms and legs with a kitchen knife.

It is a common clinical experience that certain clients appear to deteriorate or "get worse"—despite initial improvement—during abuse-focused therapy. As I have noted elsewhere, this process need not necessarily mean that therapy is deleterious or that, in fact, the client is experiencing a decompensation of any sort (Briere, 1989). Instead, such exacerbation can reflect clinical improvement. As treatment progresses, dissociative and avoidant defenses such as repression, numbing, denial, intellectualization, and tension reduction may decrease, leading to more direct awareness and experiencing of childhood injury. As a result of this improved ability to confront abuse-related issues and experiences, some clients experience more acute anxiety, depression, flashbacks, intrusive memories, and nightmares than they did prior to (or earlier in) treatment. These phenomena, in turn, may motivate a return to higher levels of tension-reduction and avoidance behaviors such as self-mutilation, bulimic activity, or substance abuse.

Such exacerbation can be unnerving to both client and therapist. For the client, this process may appear to be evidence that, in fact, his or her greatest fear is coming true: that the direct experience of formerly repressed or avoided abuse trauma is dangerous, leading to loss of control, engulfment in pain, and, perhaps, impending psychosis. The client may further assume that this seeming downturn reflects the hopelessness of ever "getting better" and, in fact, his or her undeservingness of improvement. As a result, some survivors may consider dropping out of treatment or, at minimum, may reduce the pace or intensity of treatment through distraction or avoidance activities ("resistance").

The clinician, on the other hand, may worry that he or she has made some sort of clinical error, and may consider taking a different therapeutic approach to the client. In general, the therapist should consider three possibilities: (a) The treatment *is* having negative effects, either by virtue of technical errors or as a result of countertransferential difficulties; (b) treatment is working, but process issues such as pacing, intensity control, or consolidation require more attention; and/or (c) therapy is proceeding as it should, and exacerbation is a natural, transitory effect of clinical improvement.

According to which of these dynamics is present, clinical intervention in treatment-based exacerbation may encompass any combination of several strategies. First, if exacerbation is a major issue, the clinician should seek out consultation with a specialist in abuse trauma. Issues for consultation might include whether the therapist is consciously or unconsciously responding to his or her own abuse-related issues (as opposed to the client's) and thereby contributing to the client's distress, whether the goals of treatment match the client's current level of functioning (e.g., whether extensive trauma resolution is being attempted in a survivor whose self issues and affect regulation skills require more immediate attention), and whether certain previously overlooked clinical techniques or approaches are indicated.

Second, exacerbation usually requires that the therapist increase his or her normalization and validation activities. The notion of sometimes having to get "worse" before one can get "better" may be introduced, and the positive reframe that such increased difficulties are a sign of growth and clearer perception is usually offered. Client tendencies to catastrophize are directly addressed, and any evidence of clinical improvement (e.g., less dissociation, occasional periods of higher-than-normal functioning, or greater self-awareness) is emphasized.

Third, as suggested in Chapter 6, the therapist should consider decreasing the pace and intensity of abuse-focused interventions at times when the client is besieged with painful affects and intrusive experiences. This does not mean that the clinician should stop addressing abuse issues per se, only that he or she should pay more attention to (a) titrating treatment to a level that the survivor can tolerate without overwhelming distress, (b) providing closure and dearousal whenever possible, and (c) working to consolidate previous gains and insights rather than focusing exclusively on new exploration.

Although treatment-related exacerbation is usually considered when a client experiences a dramatic and sustained increase in distress, lesser levels of exacerbation probably occur for most abuse survivors in treatment. The intensity of exacerbation in any given instance appears to be related to the extent of pretreatment denial, repression, or other avoidance (Briere, 1989). For this reason, it is recommended that all survivors in therapy be advised of the possibility of some temporary increase in difficulties as treatment progresses. This will both (a) prepare the survivor beforehand, thereby potentially decreasing the impact of exacerbation, and normalizing its presence if and when it occurs, and (b) give the client the opportunity to render informed consent to treatment, having been apprised directly that increased distress during therapy might occur (Lloyd, 1991).

☐ Substance-Addicted Survivors

Manuel

Manuel presents to an outpatient clinic with complaints of poor memory, impaired concentration, and insomnia. These difficulties are soon linked to Manuel's extensive substance abuse history: He has been drinking beer and whisky on a daily (almost hourly) basis for almost 15 years, augmented with cocaine and marijuana "whenever I can get it." Although Manuel denies any memories of a child abuse history, his brother describes severe physical abuse of both himself and Manuel by their father until early adolescence. Because he refuses to attend a chemical dependency or 12-step program,

Manuel is unsuccessful in reducing or terminating his daily substance use. This continued intoxication, in turn, has thus far prevented Manuel from entering the clinic's abuse-focused treatment program, which has a sobriety requirement.

As noted at various times in this book, child abuse survivors are more likely to become dependent on drugs or alcohol than are individuals without abuse histories, usually as a defense against abuse-related dysphoria and/or intrusive experiences. This association can lead to a circular dilemma during abuse-focused therapy: The survivor's chronic self-medication with psychoactive substances can impede treatment by blocking abuse-related memories and affects, and an abuse history may interfere with the survivor's response to standard chemical dependency treatment, including her or his ability to remain drug or alcohol abstinent. This reciprocating interference can be so problematic that some therapists refuse to treat chemically dependent survivors, and some chemical dependency programs report significantly less success in helping those who were severely abused as children.

Although it is probably an unfair practice to screen substance-abusing survivors from treatment, it is nevertheless true that abuse-focused therapy alone can be impeded dramatically when the client is substance dependent. Most abuse specialists, for example, have found that sexual abuse survivors who regularly use cocaine or heroin, or who are alcoholic, are effectively (albeit temporarily) anesthetized against abuse-related pain, and may have very little access to abuse-related memories. As a result, they may lack the motivation to address childhood maltreatment issues directly and, even when motivated, may be unable to process abuse-specific memories and affects effectively. Instead, the therapist may end up responding to one alcohol- or drug-related crisis after another, following the client from periods of denial and numbing to episodes of self-disgust, remorse, and depression.

Given the seriousness of substance addiction vis-à-vis treatment outcome, most survivors of severe abuse (especially those who were repeatedly sexually abused) should be referred for assistance in this area prior to (or concurrent with) abuse-focused psychotherapy. Such referral may be to either a 12-step program (e.g., Alcoholics Anonymous or Narcotics Anonymous) or a chemical dependency program. In the former case, the clinician should be conversant with the 12 steps of AA and their implications for treatment. While being careful not to undercut the most helpful components of these programs, such as peer support and systematic confrontation of the negative impacts of substance abuse, the therapist may wish to discuss with the client such AA concepts as "moral inventory" and "making amends," expectations that sometimes indirectly contradict the goals of abuse-focused psychotherapy.

Alternatives to AA meetings may be found in the chemical dependency programs offered by many private hospitals and residential treatment facilities. Although these programs often draw upon the AA model, and may hold AA meetings during treatment, they typically provide additional therapeutic services for the addict or alcoholic. Most of these programs occur in inpatient or residential settings, where the client receives 24-hour care and supervision. For the survivor whose substance dependency is not responsive to AA meetings alone, or whose ability to stop using drugs or alcohol is not great, such inpatient settings can be helpful. They provide greater structure, more intensive contact, and the opportunity to examine psychological issues missed by AA meetings alone. To the extent that they overlook child abuse trauma, however, their impacts may be transitory—often resulting in temporary abstinence, but typically failing to resolve the pain that motivated the substance abuse in the first place (Conte & Corwin, 1991). In the absence of trauma resolution, the survivor may easily return to familiar tension-reduction or avoidance devices, including alcohol and/or drugs.

Recognizing the importance of both child abuse *and* drug or alcohol issues, a small number of chemical dependency programs address both concerns during treatment. Although empirical data are scarce in this area, anecdotal information suggests that such programs may be considerably more helpful for abuse survivors than other kinds of programs. This potential success is likely to relate to two phenomena: attention to avoidance dynamics and negotiation of abstinence issues.

As indicated in Chapter 6, an appreciation of tension reduction, affect regulation, and avoidance dynamics allows the therapist to understand seemingly self-destructive behaviors, such as excessive drug or alcohol use. It has been suggested that such behaviors will not be easily abandoned by the survivor unless one or both of two conditions occur: (a) The survivor has access to other activities that also reduce abuse-related dysphoria, posttraumatic symptoms, and emptiness, or (b) these painful states are reduced and/or better tolerated as a result of abuse-focused therapy. Successful chemical dependency programs attempt to address both goals. For example, the survivor may be taught to use relaxation procedures, exercise, grounding, distraction, and other distress-reducing techniques described in Chapter 6 and elsewhere (e.g., Bass & Davis, 1986; Briere, 1989; Gil, 1983) when confronted with intrusive experiences or periods of extreme dysphoria. Perhaps even more important, the survivor is offered the opportunity to address critical aspects of his or her abuse history, so that drugs or alcohol are less needed to reduce painful internal experience. Treatment for abuse trauma in chemical dependency programs typically draws on the same principles and methodologies outlined in this book, except that the interventions may be more intensive, of shorter duration, and much more reliant on follow-up psychotherapy.

In order for abuse-focused treatment to succeed, however, the survivor must be substance abstinent, or at least must greatly reduce her or his drug/alcohol usage. Unfortunately, abstinence is frequently a highly stressful and threatening state for survivors who use psychoactive substances to suppress memories and distress. Beyond any physical responses to chemical dependency, the survivor may experience a growing psychological hunger for the calming and numbing effects of drugs and/or alcohol, especially upon exposure to abuse-related affects, restimulating interpersonal events, and posttraumatic intrusion. This risk of relapse upon the resurgence of (previously dampened) postabuse trauma is well known in AA circles and chemical dependency programs. In fact, the threat to abstinence entailed in confronting one's abuse is often a major concern for substance-abstinent survivors who are considering abuse-focused psychotherapy.

Because abstinence and therapy may be seemingly antagonistic events early in treatment, many clinicians recommend that either (a) abuse-focused chemical dependency treatment initially take place in an inpatient setting, where the survivor cannot gain access to drugs or alcohol without considerable difficulty, or (b) the survivor be abstinent for a reasonable period of time before abuse issues are directly addressed in therapy. In the latter case, the goal is for the survivor to become sufficiently stable in his or her sobriety that any restimulation of abuse trauma that occurs does not precipitate a return to substance use. As noted by Corwin, the actual period of sobriety required may vary from case to case (Conte & Corwin, 1991). Too short an abstinence period, for example, may result in the survivor's reinvolvement in substance abuse, whereas too long a period without attention to abuse issues may leave some survivors feeling discounted and silenced in their desire to delve into childhood trauma.

❑ **The Amnestic Abuse Survivor**

Andrew

Although he has almost no memories of his biological father, Andrew brings to the consultation session several documents that recount his physical, sexual, and psychological maltreatment as a 4-year-old by this man. One is an old newspaper clipping describing how a small child with Andrew's name was found by police, bound at the hands, with burn marks and bruises over much of his body. Andrew requests hypnosis or a Pentothal interview, stating that "it's the only way I can get myself to remember."

Most abuse-specialized psychotherapists have worked with one or more clients whose clinical presentation was highly suggestive of a sexual or physical abuse history, but who steadfastly denied any such childhood experiences. Although it is possible in any given case that no abuse in fact occurred, research on the incidence of sexual abuse-related amnesia suggests that some proportion of psychotherapy clients do in fact present with repressed abuse histories (Briere & Conte, in press; Herman & Schatzow, 1987). As described earlier, amnesia appears to be more likely if the abuse occurred early in childhood and involved relatively high levels of violence or trauma.

Clinical experience with survivors who have recovered memories suggests that abuse-amnestics tend to present with some combination or subset of several characteristics, despite their conscious experience that no abuse occurred. These can include the following, although none of these is in and of itself an inevitable indicator of amnesia:

- reports of long "blanks" in memories of childhood
- extensive use of alcohol or drugs, bulimia, and/or self-mutilation, either currently or in the past
- unexplained sexual dysfunction, intrusive negative thoughts or feelings during sex, and/or indiscriminate sexual activity that appears to have a compulsive quality
- chronic dissociation, perhaps especially depersonalization and detachment/numbing
- repetitive intrusive dreams of childhood violence that somehow seem more "real" to the survivor than other dreams
- episodes of intense, free-floating anxiety, often accompanied by depression or emptiness
- a brittle or fragile interpersonal style in which denial is used as a method of anxiety reduction

The above features are not always present, however; it is not uncommon to hear of individuals who report few or none of these specific elements, yet who eventually uncover abuse memories during therapy. Such people may appear as quite happy to others, and may be highly invested in self-determination and external success. For example, Marilyn Van Derbur, who was Miss America in 1958, revealed in 1991 that she had been sexually abused by her father from ages 5 to 18, but that she was amnestic for the event until her mid-20s. *People* magazine (June 10, 1991) quotes her as follows:

> In order to survive, I split into a day child, who giggled and smiled, and a night child, who lay awake in a fetal position, only to be pried apart by my father. Until I was 24, the day child had no conscious knowledge of the night child. . . . Anyone who knew me would say I was the happiest child. *I* believed I was happy. Still, incest colored every aspect of my life. I couldn't stand to play with dolls. Nor did I like to be touched or hugged. I also had a need to excel, to have some control over my life. I was an AAU swimmer, a skier and a golfer. I got straight A's in school. (p. 90)

As might be predicted, it is often difficult to provide abuse-specific therapy to individuals who cannot recall abuse experiences and who, in fact, may steadfastly refuse to consider consciously that abuse ever occurred. The therapist may feel caught between the need to provide treatment for what appears to be abuse trauma and the lack of any known abuse to address. Fortunately, psychotherapy that provides noncontingent support, exploration of early memories (per se), intervention in dissociative avoidance, and emotional processing of painful events often creates the requisite conditions for eventual memory recovery. In some sense, therefore, the best response of the therapist to abuse amnesia may be to provide the same sorts of interventions and support that have been outlined in this book, except that specific references to abuse episodes are obviously impossible unless or until memories begin to return.

Assuming that the clinician chooses to provide abuse-relevant therapy, regardless of formal abuse disclosure, the issue arises regarding whether or not to share this fact with the client. Although an argument can be made for silence here, little can be hurt and, ultimately, much may be gained if the therapist shares with the client his or her suspicions regarding the client's childhood experience. Obviously, however, it is not appropriate for the clinician to inform a client authoritatively that he or she was abused as a child and is repressing it. Among other possibilities, the therapist may be wrong; the client's difficulties may not, in fact, relate to repressed, severe, childhood maltreatment. Further, such a statement shows little respect for the client's sense of self-determination or unconscious decision making. Although each therapist will wish to approach this issue in his or her own way, the following example may serve as a guide:

> Beatriz, it sounds like some of the problems you describe have been around for a long time, maybe since you were a child. There are many ways that you could have ended up with these difficulties. I want to share with you one of my guesses about this. It seems to me that when you talk about _____ , one of the ways that people have that kind of problem is if they were hurt somehow when they were kids. I know that you don't remember anything happening like that, and maybe nothing like that did happen. It is possible, though, that your childhood has something to do with this. That's why, if it's okay with you,

I'll want us to explore your early memories and feelings now and then during therapy, so that we can see where _____ might have come from, and why it's still here now. How do you feel about doing that?

❑ Hospitalization

Because survivors of severe abuse can present with especially high levels of posttraumatic stress, depression, or self-destructive behavior, the question of psychiatric hospitalization occasionally arises. As is the case with hospitalization in any mental health context, the issue concerns the potential benefits of a protected, sometimes intensive treatment environment versus the possibility of iatrogenic effects: most typically stigmatization, support for dependency and/or regression, and hospital staff interference in (or contradiction of) abuse-focused psychotherapy.

All things being equal, clinical interventions that avoid the need for psychiatric hospitalization are usually preferable to those requiring inpatient admission. One of the most basic of treatment philosophies presented in Chapter 4 is that abuse-focused psychotherapy validates, respects, and promotes growth, as opposed to implying rehabilitation or recovery from a disorder. Although not all inpatient units utilize a strict disease model of intervention, it is relatively unusual to see hospital programs that convey or reinforce the perspective outlined in this book. In the worst case, survivors have been told by medical or nursing staff that their child abuse reports are lies or fantasies, that they should put their abuse behind them and stop feeling sorry for themselves, or that their abuse-related concerns are manipulative attempts to avoid confronting their actual psychiatric disorders. Furthermore, by virtue of their need to provide diagnosis and medical treatment, traditional psychiatric units often risk stigmatizing survivors with labels such as borderline or histrionic personality disorder, and tend to utilize more authoritarian interventions with such "illnesses."

Exceptions to this generalization abound, however. Inpatient psychiatric hospitalization can be indicated in two broad areas: to intervene in abuse-related emergencies such as suicidality or severe exacerbation (e.g., dissociative "catatonia," especially extreme self-mutilation, or a reactive psychosis), or to provide intensive abuse-focused treatment in less acute situations where continuous support and structure are nevertheless indicated. As noted below, to be maximally helpful such inpatient milieus must be responsive to survivor issues and needs.

Because severe child abuse experiences can be associated with later suicidality, substance abuse, revictimization, and the more self-injurious tension-reduction behaviors, it is not uncommon for survivors of such abuse to require emergency mental health services. As indicated in one study, for example, fully 70% of women without organic or psychotic disorders who presented to an urban psychiatric emergency room reported having been sexually abused as children (Briere & Zaidi, 1989). Among the *abuse-related* difficulties that I have encountered as an emergency room/trauma psychologist are severe panic episodes; recent suicide attempts and/or current suicidal intent; major depression; exacerbated PTSD symptoms (especially repetitive flashbacks); extremely chaotic and injurious relationships that lead to dramatic, self-destructive behavior; revictimization by battery or rape; brief, very intense dissociative states whose autism and bizarreness mimic psychosis; brief psychotic episodes following major restimulation events; extreme trauma after being notified of HIV or AIDS status secondary to IV drug abuse and/or unsafe sexual practices; and organic mental disorders (e.g., dementia, hallucinosis, organic delusionality) arising from chronic substance abuse.

Although not all of the above situations require more than careful outpatient crisis intervention, many do necessitate inpatient treatment. Ideally, emergency hospitalization provides safety from self-injurious impulses and the actions of malicious others (e.g., battering spouses), intensive support and reassurance, improved psychosocial assessment, medical diagnosis and treatment where indicated, adequate food and sleep, assistance with outside agencies (e.g., victims' assistance programs, welfare, probation departments), relationship/family counseling to ameliorate existing interpersonal stressors, and appropriate follow-up referrals for psychotherapy and/or self-help support groups. Equally as important as what treatment staff should do, however, is what they must not do—that is, stigmatize or belittle the survivor, use medications inappropriately (e.g., neuroleptic for nonpsychotic states, or chronic high-dosage anxiolytics for posttraumatic symptoms), use restraints or seclusion beyond what is absolutely required, or hospitalize beyond the shortest period necessary to stabilize and maintain the survivor's safety.

Recently, a number of psychiatric hospitals have developed specific inpatient units and programs for adolescent and adult sexual abuse survivors. These programs are characterized by their focus on less acute concerns—offering a safe, structured environment where survivors can address their more long-term abuse-related difficulties and issues. Typically, these units serve individuals with multiple personality disorder or other severe dissociative symptoms, chronic self-mutilation or suicidality, and/or "addictions" to drugs, food, gambling, and so on. The length of stay on these units may range from several weeks to many months, and treatment usually consists of daily individual, group, and milieu therapy.

Because they are a relatively new development, there are limited data on the effectiveness of such programs. Some survivors report important positive outcomes, such as the integration of multiple personalities, sustained abstinence from destructive tension reduction or "addictions," and significant improvements in their interpersonal functioning. A frequent comment is that such programs allow survivors temporarily to put on hold their usual daily concerns and distractions, thereby allowing them to devote sustained and focused attention to abuse-related issues. Other survivors, however, report that some "specialized" programs are no more than traditional psychiatric units that have found a new marketing technique to increase their daily census. Additional complaints have been that extended inpatient programs tend to increase dependency and avoidance of real-life concerns; that some units rely heavily on 12-step programs, thereby alienating those who do not wish a Western religious influence or group confrontation focus in their treatment plan; and that the treatment staff in some hospitals are relatively inexperienced or misinformed regarding abuse-focused psychotherapy.

Many of these differences of opinion may reflect the differing quality of treatment programs and their staffs, rather than the advantages and disadvantages of inpatient treatment per se. Such programs are more likely to be helpful if they involve well-trained treatment staff with extensive experience in abuse trauma, intervention systems well grounded in the principles and philosophy of abuse-focused therapy, and treatment plans that do not foster unnecessary dependency or regression. Additionally, such programs appear more relevant to survivors whose issues transcend those of the average survivor in therapy, that is, involving major dissociative disturbance or chronic dependence on self-destructive tension-reduction behaviors. Because of this limitation, inpatient programs should not be presented to the public as a remedy for the difficulties of every abuse survivor.

❏ Client Gender and Abuse Trauma

Janet and Ray

Janet and Ray are brother and sister, ages 16 and 15, respectively. Both are in therapy at a specialized sexual abuse treatment center following their father's conviction on nine counts of molestation and sodomy. Staff at the center often remark on the different ways in which the two appear to have dealt with their sexual abuse. Janet is working hard in therapy, and continues to do relatively well in school. She expresses more concern about Ray than about her own abuse-related difficulties, which include sexual preoccupation, self-mutilation, and flashbacks of rape. Ray, on the other hand, rarely arrives for his therapy appointments, has been expelled from school twice this year for skipping class and for fighting with schoolmates, and appears to be psychologically dependent on marijuana. In his last session, Ray described fantasies of killing and dismembering his father and escaping with his sister to another country.

Because of the many differences in the training and treatment of males and females in our society, abuse-focused psychotherapy must address gender-related issues. Although current evidence suggests that sexual abuse trauma may occur at about equivalent levels for both sexes (e.g., Briere et al., 1988; Conte, Briere, & Sexton, 1989b; Urquiza & Crowley, 1986)[1], it is clear that sex role socialization affects how such injuries are experienced and expressed. Research on male and female sex roles indicates that women are socialized to express directly certain feelings, such as fear or sadness, but are taught to dampen other affects, such as anger (e.g., Hoyenga & Hoyenga, 1979). Men, on the other hand, may be permitted the expression of anger, but are discouraged from communicating the "softer" feelings of sadness or fear. The sexes also appear to differ in how they act upon feelings and needs: Men, for example, are to some extent taught to externalize unpleasant feelings, and to act on the environment in order to reduce pain or distress (David & Brannon, 1976); women, in contrast, are generally socialized to turn such feelings inward, or at least to refrain from acting them out on others (Chesler, 1972). Probably because of these sex role prescriptions, it is not uncommon to find research reporting greater abuse-related aggression toward self (e.g., self-mutilation) in women (Briere, Henschel, Smiljanich, & Morlan-Magallanes, 1990), and more abuse-related aggression toward others (e.g., assaults) in men (Stukas-Davis, 1990).

These differences in symptom expression and behavioral response often manifest themselves during abuse-focused psychotherapy. All things being equal, for example, male abuse survivors in treatment may be more prone to expressions of anger or the intellectualization of posttraumatic distress than are female survivors, whereas formerly abused women may more frequently focus on feelings of sadness, humiliation, or helplessness. As a result, the two sexes may benefit from differential therapeutic interventions regarding the expression and catharsis of abuse-related emotions. Generally, this difference involves (a) even more clinical attention to anger ventilation and assertive responses for female survivors than for male survivors, and (b) even greater therapeutic exploration of sadness and fear (without reflexive externalization) for males than for females. This generalization does not hold for all survivors, of course, nor does it remotely imply that, for example, males should not address anger and females should avoid expressing fear or sadness. Instead, the clinician is advised to be aware of ways in which sex role socialization can suppress certain affective responses to trauma—responses that should be directly addressed during abuse-focused treatment. Additionally, given the tendency for males and females to deal with painful affects differently—that is, in terms of externalizing or internalizing distress—attention to sex role issues in treatment may help prevent or reduce injurious gender-specific tension-reduction activities.

Treatment should also address sex differences in how child abuse is cognitively processed. Because boys and men are expected to be strong and aggressive, victimization may be more of a sex role violation for them than it is for girls and women (Elliott & Briere, 1991b). This additional trauma can result in somewhat different cognitive responses to abuse for male and female survivors. Physically abused males, for example, often present with feelings of inadequacy and desire for retribution, as though a boy's inability to fight off maltreatment reflects lesser masculinity in adolescence or adulthood (Briere, 1989; Courtois, 1988). Many sexually abused males have sexual concerns related to their molestation (Courtois, 1988; Dimock, 1988; Stukas-Davis, 1990). Heterosexual boys and men may believe that childhood sexual abuse by another male has caused them to be latently homosexual—a fear that, in a culture as homophobic as ours, may result in compensatory hypermasculinity or overinvolvement in heterosexual activity. Conversely, homosexual men who were sexually abused by males may be concerned that their sexual orientation somehow caused them to be abused by men, or that their abuse caused them to be homosexual—conclusions that can lead to feelings of guilt, shame, and self-betrayal (Elliott & Briere, 1991b). (For additional information on men's processing of abuse issues, see Hunter, 1990; Lew, 1990.)

Female abuse survivors may also fear that they in some way enticed their abusers into molesting them—a concern that appears to reflect the stereotype of females as sex objects and as almost inherently seductive. This fear may be exacerbated when the sexually abused girl had learned before the abuse to behave in a "cute" or "flirtatious" manner in order to gain male attention. As a result, she may falsely interpret her pseudosexual behavior as having caused or provoked her molestation.

Because of these different cognitive sequelae, clinicians may find it advantageous to approach male and female abuse survivors in slightly different ways during treatment. Males, for example, may require additional reassurance that they are not less masculine (regardless of sexual orientation) by virtue of having been abused, and that they do not have to prove their identity through compensatory aggression. Female survivors, on the other hand, may especially benefit from interventions that support assertiveness and help them to reject feelings of responsibility for their abuse. In each case, the ultimate therapeutic goal remains the working through of abuse trauma, taking into account ways in which gender socialization may alter or exacerbate such injuries.

❏ Abuse-Related Countertransference: The Therapist Survivor

Given the incidence data presented in Chapter 1, one would expect as high a prevalence of child abuse and neglect histories among psychotherapists as in any other group in the general population. Recent research by Elliott (1990), in fact, suggests that clinicians are even more likely than other professionals to have been sexually and/or physically abused, and to have come from homes where one or both parents had problems with substance abuse.

An obvious concern is that unresolved child abuse issues can misdirect or impede the therapist's work with clients—perhaps especially clients who are abuse survivors themselves. Also worthy of attention, however, are the potentially positive contributions of survivorhood to the clinician's work with other survivors. By virtue of having "been there," the therapist who has worked through and come to terms with his or her own abuse history may be optimally suited to provide sensitive, nondiscounting services to other survivors. In fact, the survivor-therapist may be able to understand the survivor-client's experience and responses in ways that the therapist with no such history rarely can. It is probably true, in this regard, that some of the very best abuse-focused psychotherapists are survivors who have addressed and integrated their own early histories.

Because childhood abuse is so common among psychotherapists, there are a number of potential implications of such histories for countertransference. Three impediments to effective therapeutic functioning are especially relevant to the therapist who has not resolved his or her childhood history: overidentification, projection, and boundary confusion.

OVERIDENTIFICATION

Overidentification occurs when the therapist's empathic response to a client is unconsciously intensified by his or her own abuse-related affects and cognitions. As a result of these unresolved issues, the therapist "overreacts" to those aspects of the client's situation most reminiscent of his or her own experience. For example, the therapist with untreated sexual abuse trauma might feel unusually intense anxiety, sadness, or anger when hearing the sexual abuse experiences of a client with a similar childhood. The critical issue here is not the therapist's appropriate empathy and compassion for the client, but rather the point at which the clinician's own abuse-related responses significantly add to the process.

The primary danger of overidentification is that the therapist either will become less able to provide accurate assessment and treatment, by virtue of his or her heightened responses to abuse-related issues, or will engage in dissociated caretaking behaviors—in many cases overproviding the client with those things that the therapist may not be able to offer to him- or herself. For example, the survivor-therapist may become overinvested in soothing the client, in rescuing the client from difficult situations, or in punishing the perpetrator, or may become too involved in the survivor's day-to-day life. This dynamic may be most destructive when the overidentified therapist is working with a client who has major dependency or attachment needs, since each person's abuse-related difficulties are symbiotic with the other's.

PROJECTION

In some ways similar to overidentification, abuse-related projection occurs when the therapist-survivor confuses his or her own abuse issues with those of the client's. Examples of such projection are instances in which the unconsciously angry therapist views the client as more angry than he or she actually is, the clinician perceives the client as "resistant" or "manipulative" based on the therapist's own excessive need for interpersonal control, or the therapist responds to neutral client behaviors as if they were seductive in response to his or her own unresolved sexual issues. On a milder level, the therapist may project impatience or boredom onto the client when, in fact, the therapist is having difficulties with the pace or process of therapy.

Therapist projection can be especially problematic. First, the survivor inherently relies on the clinician for objective data on "reality" inside and outside of the session. Second, the clinician must be able to assess the client's state and status accurately in order to provide relevant therapeutic interventions. To the extent that the therapist's childhood history impairs his or her ability to do either of these things, the client's progress in treatment will suffer.

BOUNDARY CONFUSION

Perhaps the most dangerous form of abuse-related countertransference is that of boundary violation. This occurs when the therapist's child abuse history prevents him or her from being able to discriminate appropriate from inappropriate interpersonal behavior—especially in terms of the limits of therapeutic propriety. Examples of therapist boundary confusion include any type of sexual behavior with clients, obviously inappropriate personal disclosures during therapy, excessively intrusive questions or statements, and, most generally, the therapist's use of the client to gratify the therapist's own needs.

Not all of these examples necessarily represent boundary *confusion*, of course. A small minority of "therapists" appear to be completely aware of and able to control their exploitive behavior, yet intentionally engage in such actions. Such (hopefully rare) individuals are not involved in countertransference per se, but rather solely in immoral and often illegal behavior. When boundary violation is countertransferential, on the other hand, it is often not recognized as inappropriate at the time by the therapist, and/or may be seen by the clinician as out of his or her control.

Depending on the extent of violation involved, boundary confusion can range from nontherapeutic to tragically destructive. At minimum, any boundary incursion by the therapist is liable to restimulate and reinforce abuse-related issues and trauma in the survivor-client, and may potentially prevent or destroy the development of trust in the therapeutic relationship. At the most extreme end of the violation continuum, recent research by Magana (1990) and others clearly suggests that sexual abuse survivors who are sexually revictimized by their therapists suffer greater symptomatology than their (already symptomatic) cohorts who were molested as children but not during therapy. Less obvious victims of clinician boundary violations—such as those repeatedly exposed to therapists' intrusive questions or inappropriate statements—suffer as well, either via a resurgence in postabuse trauma or in terms of being deprived of a safe therapeutic environment.

ADDRESSING ABUSE-RELATED COUNTERTRANSFERENCE

Because of the critical importance of therapist objectivity and trustworthiness in work with child abuse survivors, countertransference must be addressed rigorously by clinicians and clinical supervisors. Although lower levels of overidentification and projection may respond to clinical vigilance alone, higher levels of these problems and almost any form of boundary confusion typically require outside intervention.

As I have noted in *Therapy for Adults Molested as Children*, work with clients who are survivors of child abuse trauma is inherently stressful, likely to pull on therapists' unresolved childhood issues, and devoid of some of the supports found in more traditional therapeutic constellations (Briere, 1989). Summit (1988) asserts in this regard that "the usual anchors of training, authority, wisdom, and professional standards are elusive and contradictory for the sexual abuse specialist" (p. 2). As a result, regular consultation (or supervision, in training contexts) is an important component of abuse-focused psychotherapy. Such support allows therapists to share the burden of daily exposure to others' pain, as well as to explore ways in which their own childhood issues may distort perception and practice in their work with clients. Many instances of overidentification or projection can be remediated by the consistent availability of a compassionate, objective consultant who is alert to countertransferential issues.

As important as consultation is, the therapist's own psychotherapy can be an especially efficient way to address the roots of abuse-related countertransference. In fact, it is likely that some proportion of survivor-therapists virtually require their own psychotherapy before they can work effectively with other abuse survivors. As noted earlier, such attention to abuse resolution not only reduces the therapist's own abuse-related difficulties, but also may result in an extraordinary psychotherapist—one who has directly experienced both childhood injury and adult growth and integration.

Abuse-related boundary confusion involving sexual behavior or other client exploitation is of sufficient gravity that it requires the individual to (a) remove him- or herself from the practice of psychotherapy, (b) refer his or her clients (especially those he or she has maltreated) to another clinician, and (c) notify relevant professional and legal authorities. Less obvious boundary confusion may justify less serious actions; nevertheless, the clinician should seek objective consultation from another professional to determine the extent of the difficulty and the most appropriate intervention(s).

❏ Note

1. Interestingly, Briere et al. (1992) report significant sex differences on the Trauma Symptom Inventory. It may be that this measure is more sensitive to gender-related phenomena than other symptom checklists.

Summary

This book has outlined the known incidence and long-term effects of a variety of types of child maltreatment, and has described a multimodal treatment approach that may be helpful in the resolution of postabuse trauma in older adolescents and adults. The intent has been to summarize what we know thus far, and to suggest some theoretical notions that may presage future work in this area. The treatment of childhood maltreatment effects is still in its infancy, however. It is likely that the next decade will bring with it a burgeoning of treatment techniques and approaches relevant to child abuse sequelae. As this field develops, so too grows the opportunity for clinicians to provide increasingly more effective services to abuse survivors. To the extent that child abuse trauma underlies a significant proportion of modern mental health problems, these developments are likely to have substantial implications for mental health practice in the years to come.

By virtue of its attention to the resolution of long-term abuse effects, this volume may inadvertently convey the notion that the

163

most we can do for child abuse victims and survivors is to treat their wounds and foster their continued growth and development. This is, of course, a critically important task. Child abuse is largely a social phenomenon, however, not an unavoidable natural catastrophe. We must not avoid the most important intervention of all: prevention of the abuse and neglect of our children and creation of an environment where all people can thrive without fear of injury from others.

Appendix:
The Child Maltreatment
Interview Schedule

The following schedule may be used for either clinical assessment or research on child abuse. When used as a clinical interview, the questions may be paraphrased as needed, and additional information may be added within the "further information" brackets. When this schedule is to be used as a research instrument, the "further information" sections should be deleted from each item, along with the topic headings (e.g., "Parental Physical Availability," "Sexual Abuse"). An abridged version of this schedule, for research only, is available from the author.

I Parental Physical Availability

1. Did your natural (biological) mother live with you until you were at
   least 16? yes _____ no _____
   If not, how old were you when she stopped being present?
   _____ years old
   [Check here if she was never present: _____]
   Why did she stop being present:
     death _____
     illness (psychiatric or physical) _____
     separation or divorce _____
     other _____ (reason: _____)
   [further information:

   _____
   _____
   _____
   _____]

2. Did your natural (biological) father live with you until you were at
   least 16? yes _____ no _____
   If not, how old were you when he stopped being present?
   _____ years old
   [Check here if he was never present: _____]
   Why did he stop being present:
     death _____
     illness (psychiatric or physical) _____
     separation or divorce _____
     other _____ (reason: _____)
   [further information:

   _____
   _____
   _____
   _____]

3. Did you ever have a stepmother or adoptive mother? yes ___ no ___
   If yes, from what age _____ to what age _____ ?
   If more than one, list your ages for each:
     age _____ to age _____
     age _____ to age _____
   [further information:

   _____
   _____
   _____
   _____]

4. Did you ever have a stepfather or adoptive father? yes _____ no _____
   If yes, from what age _____ to what age _____ ?
   If more than one, list your ages for each:
       age _____ to age _____
       age _____ to age _____
   [further information:

   _____

   _____

   _____

   _____]

5. Did you ever have foster parents? yes _____ no _____
   If yes, from what age _____ to what age _____ ?
   If more than one, list your ages for each:
       age _____ to age _____
       age _____ to age _____
   [further information:

   _____

   _____

   _____

   _____]

6. Were you raised by any other adults? yes _____ no _____
   If yes, who? _____
   From what age _____ to what age _____ ?
   If more than one, list your ages for each:
       age _____ to age _____
       age _____ to age _____
   [further information:

   _____

   _____

   _____

   _____]

7. Did you ever live in a "group home"? yes _____ no _____
   If yes, from what age _____ to what age _____ ?
   If more than one, list your ages for each:
       age _____ to age _____
       age _____ to age _____
   [further information:

   _____

   _____

   _____

   _____]

8. Were you ever in a juvenile detention facility (e.g., "juvenile hall" or
"youth authority")? yes _____ no _____
If yes, from what age _____ to what age _____ ?
If more than one, list your ages for each:
    age _____ to age _____
    age _____ to age _____
[further information:

_____
_____
_____
_____]

II Parental Disorder

1. Before age 17, did one of your parents or stepparents or foster parents
ever have to go into a psychiatric hospital for psychiatric problems?
yes _____ no _____
If yes, who? _____
How old were you on each occasion? _____
[further information:

_____
_____
_____
_____]

2. Other than being in a psychiatric hospital, did one of your parents or
stepparents ever receive psychotherapy or psychiatric medications
before you were 17? yes _____ no _____
If yes, who? _____
[further information:

_____
_____
_____
_____]

3. Did you ever feel you were being mistreated because of your parent
or parents having psychiatric problems before age 17?
yes _____ no _____
[further information:

_____
_____
_____
_____]

4. Before age 17, did one of your parents or stepparents or foster parents ever have problems with drugs or alcohol? yes _____ no _____
If yes, who? _____
About how old were you when it started? _____
About how old were you when it stopped? _____
[Check here if it hasn't stopped yet] _____
[further information:

_____
_____
_____]

Did this ever result in either parent having medical problems, getting divorced or separated, being fired from work, or being arrested for intoxication in public or while driving?
yes _____ no _____

Did you ever feel you were being mistreated because of your parent or parents' drug or alcohol problems before age 17?
yes _____ no _____
[further information:

_____
_____
_____]

5. Before age 17, did you ever see one of your parents hit or beat up your other parent? yes _____ no _____

If yes, how many times can you recall this happening? _____ times
Did your father ever hit your mother? yes _____ no _____
Did your mother ever hit your father? yes _____ no _____
Did one or more of these times result in someone bleeding, needing medical care, or the police being called? yes _____ no _____
[further information:

_____
_____
_____]

III Parental Psychological Availability

1. On average, *before age 8*, how much did you feel that your *father/step-father/foster father* loved and cared about you?

   Not at All   Very Much
       1   2   3   4

   [further information:

   _____

   _____

   _____

   _____]

2. On average, *before age 8*, how much did you feel that your *mother/step-mother/foster mother* loved and cared about you?

   Not at All   Very Much
       1   2   3   4

   [further information:

   _____

   _____

   _____

   _____]

3. On average, *from age 8 through age 16*, how much did you feel that your *father/stepfather/foster father* loved and cared about you?

   Not at All   Very Much
       1   2   3   4

   [further information:

   _____

   _____

   _____

   _____]

4. On average, *from age 8 through age 16*, how much did you feel that your *mother/stepmother/foster mother* loved and cared about you?

   Not at All   Very Much
       1   2   3   4

   [further information:

   _____

   _____

   _____

   _____]

IV Psychological Abuse

Verbal arguments and punishment can range from quiet disagreement to yelling, insulting, and other more extreme behaviors. When you were 16 or younger, how often did the following happen to you in the *average year*? Answer for your parents or stepparents or foster parents or other adult in charge of you as a child:

	Never	Once a Year	Twice a Year	3-5 Times a Year	6-10 Times a Year	11-20 Times a Year	20+ Times a Year
1. Yell at you	0	1	2	3	4	5	6
2. Insult you	0	1	2	3	4	5	6
3. Criticize you	0	1	2	3	4	5	6
4. Try to make you feel guilty	0	1	2	3	4	5	6
5. Ridicule or humiliate you	0	1	2	3	4	5	6
6. Embarrass you in front of others	0	1	2	3	4	5	6
7. Make you feel like you were a bad person	0	1	2	3	4	5	6

[further information:

_____

_____

_____

_____]

V Physical Abuse

Before age 17, did a parent or stepparent or foster parent or other adult in charge of you as a child ever:

1. Do something on purpose to you (for example, hit or punch or cut you, or push you down) that gave you bruises or scratches, broke bones or teeth, or made you bleed? yes _____ no _____
   If yes, who did this? _____
   How often before age 17? _____ times
   How old were you the first time? _____ years
   How old were you the last time (before age 17)? _____ years
   Were the authorities (i.e., the police, child welfare) ever notified?
   yes _____ no _____
   If yes, what happened: _____
   [further information:

   _____
   _____
   _____
   _____]

2. Hurt you so badly that you had to see a doctor or go to the hospital?
   yes _____ no _____
   If yes, who did this? _____
   How often before age 17? _____ times
   How old were you the first time? _____ years
   How old were you the last time (before age 17)? _____ years
   [further information:

   _____
   _____
   _____
   _____]

Before age 17, how often *in the worst year that you can remember* were you hit or spanked by your parents or other adults?

___ never	___ 1-2 times	___ 3-5 times	___ 6-10 times
___ 11-15 times	___ 16-20 times	___ 21-30 times	
___ 31-50 times	___ 51-100 times	___ 101-200 times	
___ 201-300 times	___ 300-400 times	___ over 400 times	

VI Emotional Abuse

Before age 17, did a parent or other adult who was in charge of your care ever:

1. Lock you in a room, closet, or other small space? yes _____ no _____
   If yes, who did this? _____
   How many times before age 17? _____

2. Tie you up or chain you to something? yes _____ no _____
   If yes, who did this? _____
   How many times before age 17? _____

3. Threaten to hurt or kill you? yes _____ no _____
   If yes, who did this? _____
   How many times before age 17? _____

4. Threaten to hurt or kill someone you cared about? yes _____ no _____
   If yes, who did this? _____
   How many times before age 17? _____

5. Threaten to hurt or kill your pet? yes _____ no _____
   If yes, who did this? _____
   How many times before age 17? _____

6. Threaten to leave you somewhere that frightened you or where you wouldn't be able to get back home? yes _____ no _____
   If yes, who did this? _____
   How many times before age 17? _____

7. Threaten to leave and never come back? yes _____ no _____
   If yes, who did this? _____
   How many times before age 17? _____
   [further information:

   _____
   _____
   _____
   _____]

VII Sexual Abuse

1. Before you were age 17, did anyone ever kiss you in a sexual way?
   yes _____ no _____
   Did this ever happen with a family member? yes _____ no _____
     If yes, with whom?_____
     At what ages? _____
   Did this ever happen with someone *5 or more years older* than you were?
   yes _____ no _____
     If yes, with whom? (check all that apply)
     _____   a friend
           (At what ages? _____)
           (How many friends? _____)
     _____   a stranger
           (At what ages? _____)
           (How many strangers? _____)
     _____   a family member
           (Who?_____)
           (At what ages? _____)
           (How many family members? _____)
     _____   a teacher, doctor, or other professional
           (Who?_____)
           (At what ages?_____)
           (How many teachers/doctors/professionals?_____)
     _____   a babysitter or nanny
           (Who?_____)
           (At what ages?_____)
           (How many babysitters or nannies?_____)
     _____   someone else not mentioned above
           (Who?_____)
           (At what ages?_____)
           (How many other people?_____)
   Did anyone ever use physical force on any of these occasions?
   yes_____ no_____
     If yes, who?_____
   About how many times were you kissed in a sexual way *by someone 5
   or more years older* before age 17? _____
   [further information:
   _____
   _____
   _____]

2. Before you were age 17, did anyone ever touch your body in a sexual way, or make you touch their sexual parts? yes_____ no_____
Did this ever happen with a family member? yes_____ no_____
    If yes, with whom? _____
    At what ages? _____
Did this ever happen with someone 5 *or more years older* than you were? yes_____ no_____
    If yes, with whom? (check all that apply)
    _____ a friend
            (At what ages?_____)
            (How many friends?_____)
    _____ a stranger
            (At what ages?_____)
            (How many strangers?_____)
    _____ a family member
            (Who?_____)
            (At what ages?_____)
            (How many family members?_____)
    _____ a teacher, doctor, or other professional
            (Who?_____)
            (At what ages?_____)
            (How many teachers/doctors/professionals?_____)
    _____ a babysitter or nanny
            (Who?_____)
            (At what ages?_____)
            (How many babysitters or nannies?_____)
    _____ someone else not mentioned above
            (Who?_____)
            (At what ages?_____)
            (How many other people?_____)

Did anyone ever use physical force on any of these occasions? yes_____ no_____
    If yes, who?_____

About how many times were you touched in a sexual way or made to touch someone else's sexual parts *by someone 5 or more years older* before age 17? _____
[further information:
_____
_____
_____
_____]

3. Before you were age 17, did anyone ever have oral, anal, or vaginal intercourse with you, or place their finger or objects in your anus or vagina? yes_____ no_____
Did this ever happen with a family member? yes_____ no_____
   If yes, with whom?_____
   At what ages? _____
Did this ever happen with someone *5 or more years older* than you were? yes_____ no_____
   If yes, with whom? (check all that apply)
   _____ a friend
       (At what ages?_____)
       (How many friends?_____)
   _____ a stranger
       (At what ages?_____)
       (How many strangers?_____)
   _____ a family member
       (Who?_____)
       (At what ages?_____)
       (How many family members?_____)
   _____ a teacher, doctor, or other professional
       (Who? _____)
       (At what ages?_____)
       (How many teachers/doctors/professionals?_____)
   _____ a babysitter or nanny
       (Who?_____)
       (At what ages?_____)
       (How many babysitters or nannies?_____)
   _____ someone else not mentioned above
       (Who?_____)
       (At what ages?_____)
       (How many other people?_____)

Did anyone ever use physical force on any of these occasions?
yes_____ no_____
If yes, who?_____

About how many times did anyone *5 or more years older* have oral, anal, or vaginal intercourse with you, or place their finger or objects in your anus or vagina before age 17? _____
[further information:

_____
_____
_____
_____]

Other information about abusive sexual contact before 17:

_____

_____

_____

_____]

VIII Ritualistic Abuse

Were there ever times when you were 16 or younger when you were tortured, repeatedly hurt, or forced to do something sexual during some sort of meeting, ritual, cult gathering, or religious activity? yes_____ no_____

If not, were you ever forced to watch this happen to somebody else?
yes_____ no_____
    If yes to either of these, how old were you when this took place?_____
    How old were you the first time? _____ the last time? _____
    How many times did it happen? _____ times
    Did this ever involve devil or Satan worship? yes_____ no_____
    [further information:

    _____

    _____

    _____

    _____]

IX Perceptions of Abuse Status

To the best of your knowledge, would you say that you were sexually abused as a child (before age 17)? yes_____ no_____

Would you say that you were physically abused as a child (before age 17)?
yes_____ no_____

Overall, how would you rate your childhood:
    Very Happy   Average   Very Unhappy
        1   2   3   4   5   6   7

References

Ainsworth, M. D. S. (1985). Patterns of infant-mother attachment: Antecedents and effects on development. *Bulletin of the New York Academy of Sciences, 61,* 771-791.

Alexander, P. C. (1992). Application of attachment theory to the study of sexual abuse. *Journal of Consulting and Clinical Psychology, 60,* 185-195.

Alexander, P. C., Neimeyer, R. A., & Follette, V. (1991). Group therapy for women sexually abused as children: A controlled study and investigation of individual differences. *Journal of Interpersonal Violence, 6,* 218-231.

American Humane Association. (1981). *National study on child neglect and reporting.* Denver: Author.

American Humane Association. (1984). *National study on child neglect and reporting.* Denver: Author.

American Psychiatric Association. (1987). *Diagnostic and statistical manual of mental disorders* (3rd ed., rev.). Washington, DC: Author.

Archibald, H. C., & Tuddenham, R. D. (1965). Persistent stress reaction after combat: A 20 year follow-up. *Archives of General Psychiatry, 12,* 475-481.

Ayalon, O., & Van Tassel, E. (1987). Living in dangerous environments. In M. R. Brassard, R. Germain, & S. N. Hart (Eds.), *Psychological maltreatment of children and youth* (pp. 171-182). New York: Pergamon.

Bagley, C., & Ramsay, R. (1986). Disrupted childhood and vulnerability to sexual assault: Long-term sequelae with implications for counseling. *Social Work and Human Sexuality, 4,* 33-48.

Bagley, C., & Young, L. (1987). Juvenile prostitution and child sexual abuse: A controlled study. *Canadian Journal of Community Mental Health, 6,* 5-26.

Bass, E., & Davis, L. (1986). *The courage to heal: A guide for women survivors of child sexual abuse.* New York: Perennial Library.

Bassuk, E. L., & Rubin, L. (1987). Homeless children: A neglected population. *American Journal of Orthopsychiatry, 57,* 279-286.

Beattie, M. (1987). *Codependent no more.* New York: Harper/Hazelden.

Beck, A. T. (1967). *Depression: Clinical, experimental, and theoretical aspects.* New York: Harper & Row.

Beck, A. T. (1976). *Cognitive therapy and the emotional disorders.* New York: International Universities Press.

Beck, A. T., & Emery, G., with Greenberg, M. (1985). *Anxiety disorders and phobias: A cognitive perspective.* New York: Basic Books.

Becker, D., Lira, E., Castillo, M. I., Gomez, E., & Kovalskys, J. (1990). Therapy with victims of political repression in Chile: The challenge of social reparation. *Journal of Social Issues, 46,* 133-149.

Becker, J., Skinner, L., Abel, G., & Treacy, E. (1982). Incidence and types of sexual dysfunctions in rape and incest victims. *Journal of Sex and Marital Therapy, 8,* 65-74.

Benson, C., & Heller, K. (1987). Factors in the current adjustment of young adult daughters of alcoholic and problem drinking fathers. *Journal of Abnormal Psychology, 96,* 305-312.

Berkowitz, A., & Perkins, H. W. (1988). Personality characteristics of children of alcoholics. *Journal of Consulting and Clinical Psychology, 56,* 206-209.

Berliner, L. (1991). Therapy with victimized children and their families. In J. N. Briere (Ed.), *Treating victims of child sexual abuse* (pp. 29-46). San Francisco: Jossey-Bass.

Blake-White, J., & Kline, C. M. (1985). Treating the dissociative process in adult victims of childhood incest. *Social Casework: The Journal of Contemporary Social Work, 66,* 394-402.

Bliss, E. L., & Jeppsen, A. (1985). Prevalence of multiple personality disorder among inpatients and outpatients. *American Journal of Psychiatry, 142,* 250-251.

Bowlby, J. (1973). *Attachment and loss: Vol. 2. Separation: Anxiety and anger.* London: Hogarth.

Bowlby, J. (1980). *Attachment and loss: Vol. 3. Loss, sadness, and depression.* New York: Basic Books.

Bowlby, J. (1982). *Attachment and loss: Vol. 1. Attachment* (2nd ed.). New York: Basic Books.

Bowlby, J. (1988). *A secure base: Parent-child attachment and healthy human development.* New York: Basic Books.

Bradshaw, J. (1988). *Healing the shame that binds you.* Deerfield Beach, FL: Health Communications.

Braun, B. G. (1988). The BASK (behavior, affect, sensation, knowledge) model of dissociation. *Dissociation, 1,* 4-23.

Briere, J. (1987). Predicting likelihood of battering: Attitudes and childhood experiences. *Journal of Research in Personality, 21,* 61-69.

Briere, J. (1988). The longterm clinical correlates of childhood sexual victimization. *Annals of the New York Academy of Sciences, 528,* 327-334.

Briere, J. (1989). *Therapy for adults molested as children: Beyond survival.* New York: Springer.

Briere, J. (1991). *The Trauma Symptom Inventory.* Unpublished psychological test, University of Southern California School of Medicine, Los Angeles.

Briere, J. (1992). Methodological issues in the study of sexual abuse effects. *Journal of Consulting and Clinical Psychology, 60,* 196-203.

Briere, J., & Conte, J. (in press). Amnesia for abuse in adults molested as children. *Journal of Traumatic Stress.*

Briere, J., Cotman, A., Harris, K., & Smiljanich, K. (1992, August). *The Trauma Symptom Inventory: Preliminary data on reliability and validity.* Paper presented at the annual meeting of the American Psychological Association, Washington, DC.

Briere, J., Evans, D., Runtz, M., & Wall, T. (1988). Symptomatology in men who were molested as children: A comparison study. *American Journal of Orthopsychiatry, 58,* 457-461.

Briere, J., Henschel, D., & Smiljanich, K. (in press). Attitudes Toward Sexual Abuse (ATSA): Sex differences and construct validity. *Journal of Research in Personality.*

Briere, J., Henschel, D., Smiljanich, K., & Morlan-Magallanes, M. (1990, April). *Self-injurious behavior and child abuse history in adult men and women.* Paper presented at the National Symposium on Child Victimization, Atlanta.

Briere, J., & Runtz, M. (1986). Suicidal thoughts and behaviours in former sexual abuse victims. *Canadian Journal of Behavioural Science, 18,* 413-423.

Briere, J., & Runtz, M. (1987). Post sexual abuse trauma: Data and implications for clinical practice. *Journal of Interpersonal Violence, 2,* 367-379.

Briere, J., & Runtz, M. (1988a). Multivariate correlates of childhood psychological and physical maltreatment among university women. *Child Abuse & Neglect, 12,* 331-341.

Briere, J., & Runtz, M. (1988b). Symptomatology associated with childhood sexual victimization in a non-clinical sample. *Child Abuse & Neglect, 12,* 51-59.

Briere, J., & Runtz, M. (1989a). The Trauma Symptom Checklist (TSC-33): Early data on a new scale. *Journal of Interpersonal Violence, 4,* 151-163.

Briere, J., & Runtz, M. (1989b). University males' sexual interest in children: Predicting potential indices of "pedophilia" in a non-forensic sample. *Child Abuse & Neglect, 13,* 65-75.

Briere, J., & Runtz, M. (1990a). Augmenting Hopkins SCL scales to measure dissociative symptoms: Data from two nonclinical samples. *Journal of Research in Personality, 55,* 376-379.

Briere, J., & Runtz, M. (1990b). Differential adult symptomatology associated with three types of child abuse histories. *Child Abuse & Neglect, 14,* 357-364.

Briere, J., & Woo, R. (1991, August). *Child abuse sequelae in adult psychiatric emergency room patients.* Paper presented at the annual meeting of the American Psychological Association, San Francisco.

Briere, J., & Zaidi, L. Y. (1989). Sexual abuse histories and sequelae in female psychiatric emergency room patients. *American Journal of Psychiatry, 146,* 1602-1606.

Brown, S. (1988). *Treating adult children of alcoholics: A developmental perspective.* New York: John Wiley.

Browne, A., & Finkelhor, D. (1986). Impact of child sexual abuse: A review of the research. *Psychological Bulletin, 99,* 66-77.

Bruch, H. (1973). *Eating disorders: Obesity, anorexia nervosa, and the person within.* New York: Basic Books.

Bryer, J. B., Nelson, B. A., Miller, J. B., & Krol, P. A. (1987). Childhood sexual and physical abuse as factors in adult psychiatric illness. *American Journal of Psychiatry, 144,* 1426-1430.

Bullard, D. M., Glasser, H. H., Hagarty, M. C., & Pivchik, E. C. (1967). Failure to thrive in the "neglected" child. *American Journal of Orthopsychiatry, 37,* 680-690.

Burgess, A. W., & Holmstrom, L. L. (1979). *Rape: Crisis and recovery.* Bowie, MD: Robert Brady.

Burt, M. R. (1980). Cultural myths and supports for rape. *Journal of Personality and Social Psychology, 38,* 217-230.

Butler, S. (1979). *Conspiracy of silence: The trauma of incest.* San Francisco: Volcano.

Carlin, A. S., & Ward, N. G. (1989, August). *Subtypes of psychiatric inpatient women who have been sexually abused.* Paper presented at the annual meeting of the American Psychological Association, New Orleans.

Chafetz, M. E., Blane, H. T., & Hill, M. J. (1971). Children of alcoholics. *Quarterly Journal of Studies on Alcohol, 32,* 687-698.

Chesler, P. (1972). *Women and madness.* New York: Axon.

Chu, J. A., & Dill, D. L. (1990). Dissociative symptoms in relation to childhood physical and sexual abuse. *American Journal of Psychiatry, 147,* 887-892.

Claydon, P. (1987). Self-reported alcohol, drug, and eating disorder problems among male and female collegiate children of alcoholics. *Journal of American College Health, 36,* 111-116.

Cloninger, C. R. (1983). Genetic and environmental factors in the development of alcoholism. In S. Blume (Ed.), Alcoholism [Special issue]. *Journal of Psychiatric Treatment Evaluation, 5,* 487ff.

Cole, C. B. (1986, May). *Differential long-term effects of child sexual and physical abuse.* Presented at the Fourth National Conference on Sexual Victimization of Children, New Orleans.

Cole, P. M., & Putnam, F. W. (1992). Effect of incest on self and social functioning: A developmental psychopathology perspective. *Journal of Consulting and Clinical Psychology, 60,* 174-184.

Conte, J., Briere, J., & Sexton, D. (1989a, August). *Moderators of the long-term effects of sexual abuse.* Paper presented at the annual meeting of the American Psychological Association, New Orleans.

Conte, J., Briere, J., & Sexton, D. (1989b, October). *Sex differences in the long-term effects of sexual abuse.* Paper presented at the Eighth National Conference on Child Abuse and Neglect, Salt Lake City.

Conte, J., & Corwin, N. (1991, July). *Common clinical errors in the treatment of adult survivors.* Workshop presented at the annual meeting of VOICES, Chicago.

Coons, P. M., & Milstead, V. (1984). Rape and post-traumatic stress in multiple personality. *Psychological Reports, 55,* 839-845.

Courtois, C. A. (1979). The incest experience and its aftermath. *Victimology: An International Journal, 4,* 337-347.

Courtois, C. A. (1988). *Healing the incest wound: Adult survivors in therapy.* New York: W. W. Norton.

Courtois, C. A. (1991). Theory, sequencing, and strategy in treating adult survivors. In J. N. Briere (Ed.), *Treating victims of child sexual abuse* (pp. 47-60). San Francisco: Jossey-Bass.

Courtois, C. A. (in press). The memory retrieval process in incest survivor therapy. *Journal of Child Sexual Abuse.*

Craine, L. S., Henson, C. H., Colliver, J. A., & MacLean, D. G. (1988). Prevalence of a history of sexual abuse among female psychiatric patients in a state hospital system. *Hospital and Community Psychiatry, 39,* 300-304.

Cunningham, J., Pearce, T., & Pearce, P. (1988). Childhood sexual abuse and medical complaints in adult women. *Journal of Interpersonal Violence, 3,* 131-144.

David, D. S., & Brannon, R. (Ed.). (1976). *The forty-nine percent majority: The male sex role.* Reading, MA: Addison-Wesley.

Davis, L. (1990). *The courage to heal workbook: For women and men survivors of child sexual abuse.* New York: Harper & Row.

Dembo, R., Williams, L., LaVoie, L., Barry, E., Getreu, A., Wish, E., Schmeider, J., & Washburn, M. (1989). Physical abuse, sexual victimization, and illicit drug use: Replication of a structural analysis among a new sample of high-risk youths. *Violence and Victims, 4,* 121-138.

Derogatis, L. R., Lipman, R. S., Rickels, K., Ulenhuth, E. H., & Covi, L. (1974). The Hopkins Symptom Checklist (HSCL): A self-report symptom inventory. *Behavioral Science, 19,* 1-15.

Dimock, P. (1988). Adult males sexually abused as children: Characteristics and implications for treatment. *Journal of Interpersonal Violence, 3,* 203-221.

Dolan, Y. M. (1991). *Resolving sexual abuse: Solution-focused therapy and Ericksonian hypnosis for adult survivors.* New York: W. W. Norton.

Egeland, B. (1989, October). *A longitudinal study of high risk families: Issues and findings.* Paper presented at the Research Forum on Issues in the Longitudinal Study of Child Maltreatment, Toronto, Ontario.

Egeland, B., & Erickson, M. (1987). Psychologically unavailable caregiving. In M. R. Brassard, R. Germain, & S. N. Hart (Eds.), *Psychological maltreatment of children and youth* (pp. 110-120). New York: Pergamon.

Egeland, B., & Farber, E. A. (1984). Infant-mother attachment: Factors related to its development and changes over time. *Child Development, 55,* 753-771.

Egeland, B., & Sroufe, L. A. (1981). Developmental sequelae of maltreatment in infancy. In R. Rinsley & D. Cicchetti (Eds.), *New directions for child development: Developmental perspectives in child maltreatment* (pp. 77-92). San Francisco: Jossey-Bass.

Egeland, B., Sroufe, L. A., & Erickson, M. (1983). The developmental consequences of different patterns of maltreatment. *Child Abuse & Neglect, 7,* 459-469.

Eisenberg, N., Owens, R. G., & Dewey, M. E. (1987). Attitudes of health professionals to child sexual abuse. *Child Abuse & Neglect, 11,* 109-116.

Elliott, D. M. (1990). *The effects of childhood sexual abuse on adult functioning in a national sample of professional women.* Unpublished doctoral dissertation, Biola University, Rosemead School of Psychology, Los Angeles.

Elliott, D. M., & Briere, J. (1991a, August). *Multivariate impacts of parental incest, physical maltreatment, and substance abuse.* Paper presented at the annual meeting of the American Psychological Association, San Francisco.

Elliott, D. M., & Briere, J. (1991b). The sexually abused boy: Problems in manhood. *Medical Aspects of Human Sexuality, 26,* 68-71.

Elliott, D. M., & Briere, J. (1991c). Studying the long-term effects of sexual abuse: The Trauma Symptom Checklist (TSC) scales. In A. W. Burgess (Ed.), *Rape and sexual assault: Vol. 3. A research handbook* (pp. 57-74). New York: Garland.

Elliott, D. M., & Briere, J. (1992). Sexual abuse trauma among professional women: Validating the Trauma Symptom Checklist-40 (TSC-40). *Child Abuse & Neglect, 16,* 391-398.

Elliott, D. M., & Edwards, K. J. (1991, August). *Individuals raised by alcoholic versus mentally ill parents: A comparison study.* Paper presented at the annual meeting of the American Psychological Association, San Francisco.

Elliott, D. M., & Gabrielson-Cabush, D. L. (1990, August). *Impaired object relations in professional women molested as children.* Paper presented at the annual meeting of the American Psychological Association, Los Angeles.

Ellis, A. (1977). The basic clinical theory of rational-emotive therapy. In A. Ellis & R. Grieger (Eds.), *Handbook of rational-emotive therapy.* New York: Springer.

Epstein, M. K., & Epstein, E. K. (1990). Codependence as social narrative. *Readings: A Journal of Reviews and Social Commentary in Mental Health, 5,* 4-7.

Erickson, M. F., Egeland, B., & Pianta, R. (1989). The effects of maltreatment on the development of young children. In D. Cicchetti & V. Carlson (Eds.), *Research and theory: Child maltreatment* (pp. 647-684). London: Cambridge University Press.

Finkelhor, D. (1979). *Sexually victimized children.* New York: Free Press.

Finkelhor, D. (1984). *Child sexual abuse: New theory and research.* New York: Free Press.

Finkelhor, D., & Browne, A. (1985). The traumatic impact of child sexual abuse: A conceptualization. *American Journal of Orthopsychiatry, 55,* 530-541.

Finkelhor, D., Hotaling, G., Lewis, I. A., & Smith, C. (1989). Sexual abuse and its relationship to later sexual satisfaction, marital status, religion, and attitudes. *Journal of Interpersonal Violence, 4,* 279-399

Finn, S. E., Hartman, M., Leon, G., & Lawson, L. (1986). Eating disorders and sexual abuse: Lack of confirmation of a clinical hypothesis. *International Journal of Eating Disorders, 5,* 1035-1050.

Fisher, P. M. (1991). *Women survivors of childhood sexual abuse: Clinical sequelae and treatment.* Unpublished doctoral dissertation, Simon Fraser University, Burnaby, British Columbia.

Follette, V. M. (1991). Marital therapy for sexual abuse survivors. In J. N. Briere (Ed.), *Treating victims of child sexual abuse* (pp. 61-72). San Francisco: Jossey-Bass.

Freud, S. (1958). *A general introduction to psychoanalysis.* New York: Pocket Books.

Freud, S. (1966). *The standard edition of the complete psychological works of Sigmund Freud* (J. Strachey, Ed. and Trans.). London: Hogarth.

Friedrich, W. N. (1990). *Psychotherapy of sexually abused children and their families.* New York: W. W. Norton.

Friedrich, W. N. (1991). Sexual behavior in sexually abused children. In J. N. Briere (Ed.), *Treating victims of child sexual abuse* (pp. 15-28). San Francisco: Jossey-Bass.

Fromuth, M. E. (1986). The relationship of childhood sexual abuse with later psychological and sexual adjustment in a sample of college women. *Child Abuse & Neglect, 10,* 5-16.

Garbarino, J., Guttman, E., & Seeley, J. (1986). *The psychologically battered child: Strategies for identification, assessment and intervention.* San Francisco: Jossey-Bass.

Gardner, A. R., & Gardner, A. J. (1975). Self-mutilation, obsessionality and narcissism. *International Journal of Psychiatry, 127,* 127-132.

Gardner, L. I. (1972). Deprivation dwarfism. *Scientific American, 227,* 76-82.

Gelinas, D. J. (1983). The persisting negative effects of incest. *Psychiatry, 46,* 312-332.

Gelles, R. J., & Straus, M. A. (1987). Is violence toward children increasing? A comparison of 1975 and 1985 national survey rates. *Journal of Interpersonal Violence, 2,* 212-222.

George, C., & Main, M. (1979). Social interactions of young abused children: Approach, avoidance and aggression. *Child Development, 50,* 306-318.

Gil, D. G. (1987). Maltreatment as a function of the structure of social systems. In M. R. Brassard, R. Germain, & S. N. Hart (Eds.), *Psychological maltreatment of children and youth* (pp. 159-170). New York: Pergamon.

Gil, E. (1983). *Outgrowing the pain: A book for and about adults abused as children.* Rockville, MD: Launch.

Gil, E. (1988). *Treatment of adult survivors of childhood abuse.* Rockville, MD: Launch.

Gold, E. R. (1986). Long-term effects of sexual victimization in childhood: An attributional approach. *Journal of Consulting and Clinical Psychology, 54,* 471-475.

Gomes-Schwartz, B., Horowitz, J. M., & Cardarelli, A. P. (1990). *Child sexual abuse: The initial effects.* Newbury Park, CA: Sage.

Goodwin, D. W. (1979). Alcoholism and heredity: A review and hypothesis. *Archives of General Psychiatry, 36,* 57-61.

Goodwin, D. W. (1984). Studies of familial alcoholism: A review. *Journal of Clinical Psychiatry, 45,* 14-17.

Goodwin, J. (1989). *Sexual abuse: Incest victims and their families* (2nd ed.). Chicago: Year Book Medical Publishers.

Goodwin, J., Attias, R., McCarty, T., Chandler, S., & Romanik, R. (in press). Effects on psychiatric inpatients of routine questioning about childhood sexual abuse. *Victimology.*

Goodwin, J., & Talwar, N. (1989). Group psychotherapy for victims of incest. *Psychiatric Clinics of North America: Treatment of Victims of Sexual Abuse, 12,* 257-278.

Graziano, A. M., & Namaste, K. A. (1990). Parental use of physical force in child discipline: A survey of 679 college students. *Journal of Interpersonal Violence, 5,* 449-463.

Greenberg, M. S., & van der Kolk, B. A. (1987). Retrieval and integration of traumatic memories with the "painting cure." In B. A. van der Kolk (Ed.), *Psychological trauma* (pp. 191-215). Washington, DC: American Psychiatric Press.

Grinker, R. R., & Spiegel, J. J. (1945). *Men under stress.* New York: McGraw-Hill.

Groves, J. E. (1975). Management of the borderline patient on a medical or surgical ward: The psychiatric consultant's role. *International Journal of Psychiatry in Medicine, 6,* 337-348.

Grunebaum, H. U., & Klerman, G. L. (1967). Wrist slashing. *American Journal of Psychiatry, 124,* 527-534.

Gunderson, J. G. (1984). *Borderline personality disorder.* Washington, DC: American Psychiatric Press.

Gunderson, J. G., & Zanarini, M. C. (1983). *Diagnostic Interview for Borderlines* (rev.). Unpublished instrument, McLean Hospital, Belmont, MA.

Hamilton, N. G. (1988). *Self and others: Object relations theory in practice.* Northvale, NJ: Aronson.

Hart, S. N., Germain, R., & Brassard, M. R. (1987). The challenge: To better understand and combat the psychological maltreatment of children and youth. In M. R. Brassard, R. Germain, & S. N. Hart (Eds.), *Psychological maltreatment of children and youth* (pp. 3-24). New York: Pergamon.

Hartman, M., Finn, S. E., & Leon, G. R. (1987). Sexual abuse experiences in a clinical population: Comparisons of familial abuse. *Psychotherapy, 24,* 154-159.

Henderson, J. (1975). Incest. In A. M. Freedman, H. I. Kaplan, & B. S. Sadock (Eds.), *Comprehensive textbook of psychiatry* (Vol. 2). Baltimore: Williams & Wilkins.

Henderson, J. L., & Moore, M. (1944). The psychoneuroses of war. *New England Journal of Medicine, 230,* 125-131.

Henschel, D., Briere, J., Magallanes, M., & Smiljanich, K. (1990, April). *Sexual abuse related attributions: Probing the role of "traumagenic factors."* Paper presented at the annual meeting of the Western Psychological Association, Los Angeles.

Herman, J. L. (1981). *Father-daughter incest.* Cambridge, MA: Harvard University Press.

Herman, J. L. (1986). Histories of violence in an outpatient population. *American Journal of Psychiatry, 56,* 137-141.

Herman, J. L., Perry, C., & van der Kolk, B. A. (1989). Childhood trauma in borderline personality disorder. *American Journal of Psychiatry, 146,* 490-494.

Herman, J. L., & Schatzow, E. (1987). Recovery and verification of memories of childhood sexual trauma. *Psychoanalytic Psychology, 4,* 1-14.

Herman, J. L., & van der Kolk, B. A. (1987). Traumatic antecedents of borderline personality disorder. In B. A. van der Kolk (Ed.), *Psychological trauma* (pp. 111-126). Washington, DC: American Psychiatric Press.

Hibbard, S. (1989). Personality and object relational pathology in young adult children of alcoholics. *Psychotherapy, 26,* 504-509.

Hilgard, E. R. (1986). *Divided consciousness: Multiple controls in human thought and action* (expanded ed.). New York: John Wiley.

Hoyenga, K. B., & Hoyenga, K. T. (1979). *The question of sex differences: Psychological, cultural, and biological issues.* Boston: Little, Brown.

Hunter, M. (1990). *Abused boys: The neglected victims of sexual abuse.* Lexington, MA: Lexington.

Jaffe, P. G., Wolfe, D. A., & Wilson, S. K. (1990). *Children of battered women.* Newbury Park, CA: Sage.

Jehu, D. (1988). *Beyond sexual abuse: Therapy with women who were childhood victims.* Chichester, UK: John Wiley.

Jehu, D., Gazan, M., & Klassen, C. (1984-1985). Common therapeutic targets among women who were sexually abused in childhood. *Journal of Social Work and Human Sexuality, 3,* 25-45.

Jones, I. H., Congin, L., Stevenson, J., Straus, N., & Frei, D. Z. (1979). A biological approach to two forms of human self-injury. *Journal of Nervous and Mental Disease, 167,* 74-78.

Jones, R. L., & Jones, J. M. (1987). Racism as psychological maltreatment. In M. R. Brassard, R. Germain, & S. N. Hart (Eds.), *Psychological maltreatment of children and youth* (pp. 146-158). New York: Pergamon.

Kaplan, S., Pelcovitz, D., Salzinger, S., & Ganeles, D. (1983). Psychopathology of parents of abused and neglected children and adolescents. *Journal of the American Academy of Child Psychiatry, 22,* 238-244.

Kearney-Cooke, A. (1988). Group treatment of sexual abuse among women with eating disorders. *Women & Therapy, 7,* 5-21.

Kempe, C. H., Silverman, F. N., Steele, B. F., Droegmuller, W., & Silver, H. K. (1962). The battered-child syndrome. *Journal of the American Medical Association, 181,* 17-24.

Kernberg, O. F. (1976). *Borderline conditions and pathological narcissism.* New York: Aronson.

Kilpatrick, D. G., Saunders, B. E., Amick-McMullan, A., Best, C. L., Veronen, L. J., & Resick, H. S. (1989). Victim and crime factors associated with the development of crime-related post-traumatic stress disorder. *Behavior Therapy, 20,* 199-214.

Kluft, R. P. (Ed.). (1985). *Childhood antecedents of multiple personality.* Washington, DC: American Psychiatric Press.

Kohut, H. (1971). *The analysis of the self.* New York: International Universities Press.

Kolb, L. C. (1984). The post-traumatic stress disorders of combat: A subgroup with a conditioned emotional response. *Military Medicine, 149,* 237-243.

Kolko, D. J., Moser, J. T., & Weldy, S. R. (1988). Behavioral/emotional indications of sexual abuse in child psychiatric inpatients: A controlled comparison with physical abuse. *Child Abuse & Neglect, 12,* 529-542.

Krier, B. A. (1990, July 29). Everyday addicts. *Los Angeles Times,* pp. E1, E10-E11.

LaBarbera, J. D., Martin, J. E., & Dozier, J. E. (1980). Child psychiatrists' view of father-daughter incest. *Child Abuse & Neglect, 4,* 147-151.

Lamb, M. E., Gaensbauer, T. J., Malkin, C. M., & Schultz, L. A. (1985). The effects of child maltreatment on security of infant-adult attachment. *Infant Behavior and Development, 8,* 35-45.

Langevin, R., Handy, L., Hook, H., Day, D., & Russon, A. (1985). Are incestuous fathers pedophilic and aggressive? In R. Langevin (Ed.), *Erotic preference, gender, identity, and aggression.* Hillsdale, NJ: Lawrence Erlbaum.

Lanktree, C. B., Briere, J., Henschel, D., Morlan-Magallanes, M., & Smiljanich, K. (1990, April). *Type and extent of child abuse history associated with pelvic complaints in university women.* Paper presented at the National Symposium on Child Victimization, Atlanta.

Lanktree, C. B., Briere, J., & Zaidi, L. Y. (1991). Incidence and impacts of sexual abuse in a child outpatient sample: The role of direct inquiry. *Child Abuse & Neglect, 15,* 447-453.

Lew, M. (1990). *Victims no longer: Men recovering from incest and other sexual child abuse.* New York: Harper Collins.

Lewis, M. (1978). *Roget's international thesaurus.* New York: Thomas Y. Crowell.

Lindberg, F. H., & Distad, L. J. (1985). Post-traumatic stress disorders in women who experienced childhood incest. *Child Abuse & Neglect, 9,* 329-334.

Lipovsky, J. A., Saunders, B. E., & Murphy, S. M. (1989). Depression, anxiety, and behavior problems among victims of father-child sexual assault and nonabused siblings. *Journal of Interpersonal Violence, 4,* 452-468.

Lloyd, D. W. (1991). Legal issues in clinical work with child sexual abuse survivors. In J. N. Briere (Ed.), *Treating victims of child sexual abuse* (pp. 73-86). San Francisco: Jossey-Bass.

Lobel, C. M. (1990). *Relationship between childhood sexual abuse and borderline personality disorder in women psychiatric inpatients.* Unpublished doctoral dissertation, California Graduate Institute, Los Angeles.

Magana, D. (1990). *The impact of client-therapist sexual intimacy and child sexual abuse on psychosexual and psychological functioning.* Unpublished doctoral dissertation, University of California, Los Angeles.

Mahler, M. S., Pine, F., & Bergman, A. (1975). *The psychological birth of the human infant.* New York: Basic Books.

Main, M., & Weston, D. R. (1981). The quality of the toddler's relationship to mother and father. *Child Development, 52,* 932-940.

Maltz, W. (1988). Identifying and treating the sexual repercussions of incest: A couples therapy approach. *Journal of Sex and Marital Therapy, 14,* 145-163.

Maltz, W. (1991). *The sexual healing journey: A guide for survivors of sexual abuse.* New York: Harper Collins.

Maltz, W., & Holman, B. (1987). *Incest and sexuality: A guide to understanding and healing.* Lexington, MA: Lexington.

Masterson, J. F. (1976). *Psychotherapy of the borderline adult: A developmental approach.* New York: Brunner/Mazel.

Masterson, J. F., & Rinsley, D. B. (1975). The borderline syndrome: The role of the mother in the genesis and psychic structure of the borderline personality. *International Journal of Psycho-Analysis, 56,* 163-177.

McCann, I. L., & Pearlman, L. A. (1990). *Psychological trauma and the adult survivor: Theory, therapy, and transformation.* New York: Brunner/Mazel.

McCord, J. (1983). A forty year perspective on effects of child abuse and neglect. *Child Abuse & Neglect, 7,* 265-270.

McCord, J. (1985). Long-term adjustment in female survivors of incest: An exploratory study. *Dissertation Abstracts International, 46,* 650B.

McLeer, S. V., Deblinger, E., Atkins, M. S., Foa, E. B., & Ralphe, D. L. (1988). Posttraumatic stress disorder in sexually abused children. *Journal of the American Academy of Child and Adolescent Psychiatry, 27,* 650-654.

Meichenbaum, D. (1977). *Cognitive-behavior modification.* New York: Plenum.

Meiselman, K. C. (1978). *Incest: A psychological study of causes and effects with treatment recommendations.* San Francisco: Jossey-Bass.

Meiselman, K. C. (1990). *Resolving the trauma of incest: Reintegration therapy with survivors.* San Francisco: Jossey-Bass.

Miller, A. (1984). *Thou shalt not be aware.* New York: Farrar, Straus, & Giroux.

Millon, J. (1983). *Millon Clinical Multiaxial Inventory* (rev. ed.). Minneapolis: Interpretive Scoring System.

Molnar, J. M., Rath, W. R., & Klein, T. P. (1990). Constantly compromised: The impact of homelessness on children. *Journal of Social Issues, 46,* 109-124.

Morrison, J. (1989). Childhood sexual histories of women with somatization disorder. *American Journal of Psychiatry, 146,* 239-241.

Murphy, J. M., Jellinek, M., Quin, D., Smith, G., Poitrast, F., & Goshko, M. (1991). Substance abuse and serious child mistreatment: Prevalence, risk, and outcome in a court sample. *Child Abuse & Neglect, 15,* 197-211.

Muuss, R. E. (1986). Adolescent eating disorder: Bulimia. *Adolescence, 21,* 257-267.

National Center on Child Abuse and Neglect. (1981). *Executive summary: National study of the incidence and severity of child abuse and neglect.* Washington, DC: Author.

National Center on Child Abuse and Neglect. (1988). *National incidence and prevalence of child abuse and neglect.* Washington, DC: Author.

Navarre, E. L. (1987). Psychological maltreatment: The core component of child abuse. In M. R. Brassard, R. Germain, & S. N. Hart (Eds.), *Psychological maltreatment of children and youth* (pp. 45-56). New York: Pergamon.

Ogata, S. N., Silk, K. R., Goodrich, S., Lohr, N. E., Westen, D., & Hill, E. M. (1990). Childhood sexual and physical abuse in adult patients with borderline personality disorder. *American Journal of Psychiatry, 147,* 1008-1013.

Parker, D. A., & Harford, T. C. (1988). Alcohol-related problems, marital disruptions and depressive symptoms among adult children of alcohol abusers in the United States. *Journal of Studies on Alcohol, 49,* 306-313.

Peele, S., & Brodsky, A., with Arnold, M. (1991). *The truth about addiction and recovery.* New York: Simon & Schuster.

Peters, S. D. (1984). *The relationship between childhood sexual victimization and adult depression among Afro-American and white women.* Unpublished doctoral dissertation, University of California, Los Angeles.

Peters, S. D. (1988). Child sexual abuse and later psychological problems. In G. E. Wyatt & G. J. Powell (Eds.), *Lasting effects of child sexual abuse* (pp. 108-118). Newbury Park, CA: Sage.

Peterson, C., & Seligman, M. E. P. (1983). Learned helplessness and victimization. *Journal of Social Issues, 39,* 103-116.

Piran, N., Lerner, P., Garfinkel, P. E., Kennedy, S. H., & Brouillette, C. (1988). Personality disorders in anorexic patients. *International Journal of Eating Disorders, 7,* 589-599.

Pollock, V. E., Briere, J., Schneider, L., Knop, J., Mednick, S. A., & Goodwin, D. W. (1990). Childhood antecedents of antisocial behavior: Parental alcoholism and physical abusiveness. *American Journal of Psychiatry, 147,* 1290-1293.

Pollock, V. E., Schneider, L. S., Gabrielli, W. F., & Goodwin, D. W. (1987). Sex of parent and offspring in the transmission of alcoholism: A meta-analysis. *Journal of Nervous and Mental Disease, 175,* 668-673.

Putnam, F. W. (1989). *Diagnosis and treatment of multiple personality disorder.* New York: Guilford.

Putnam, F. W. (1990). Disturbance of "self" in victims of childhood sexual abuse. In R. P. Kluft (Ed.), *Incest-related syndromes of adult psychopathology* (pp. 113-132). Washington, DC: American Psychiatric Press.

Putnam, F. W., Guroff, J. J., Silberman, E. K., Barban, L., & Post, R. M. (1986). The clinical phenomenology of multiple personality disorder: Review of 100 recent cases. *Journal of Clinical Psychiatry, 47,* 285-293.

Pynoos, R. S., & Eth, S. (1984). The child as witness to homicide. *Journal of Social Issues, 40,* 87-108.

Reidy, T. J. (1977). The aggressive characteristics of abused and neglected children. *Journal of Clinical Psychology, 33,* 1140-1145.

Reiker, P. P., & Carmen, E. (1986). The victim-to-patient process: The disconfirmation and transformation of abuse. *American Journal of Orthopsychiatry, 56,* 360-370.

Reschly, D. J., & Graham-Clay, S. (1987). Psychological abuse from prejudice and cultural bias. In M. R. Brassard, R. Germain, & S. N. Hart (Eds.), *Psychological maltreatment of children and youth* (pp. 137-145). New York: Pergamon.

Rescorla, L., Parker, R., & Stolley, P. (1991). Ability, achievement, and adjustment in homeless children. *American Journal of Orthopsychiatry, 61,* 210-220.

Rinsley, D. B. (1980). *Treatment of the severely disturbed adolescent.* New York: Aronson.

Rohsenow, D. J., Corbett, R., & Devine, D. (1988). Molested as children: A hidden contribution to substance abuse? *Journal of Substance Abuse, 5,* 13-18.

Rokous, F., Carter, D., & Prentky, R. (1988, April). *Sexual and physical abuse in the developmental histories of child molesters.* Paper presented at the National Symposium on Child Abuse, Anaheim, CA.

Root, M. P. P., & Fallon, P. (1988). The incidence of victimization experiences in a bulimic sample. *Journal of Interpersonal Violence, 3,* 161-173.

Root, M. P. P., & Fallon, P. (1989). Treating the victimized bulimic: The functions of binge-purge behavior. *Journal of Interpersonal Violence, 4,* 90-100.

Rosenberg, M. S. (1984). *The impact of witnessing interparental violence on children's behavior, perceived competence, and social problem solving activities.* Unpublished doctoral dissertation, University of Virginia.

Rosenthal, J. A. (1988). Patterns of reported child abuse and neglect. *Child Abuse & Neglect, 12,* 263-276.

Ross, C. A. (1989). *Multiple personality disorder: Diagnosis, clinical features, and treatment.* New York: John Wiley.

Ross, C. A., Anderson, G., Fleisher, W. P., & Norton, G. R. (1991). The frequency of multiple personality disorder among psychiatric inpatients. *American Journal of Psychiatry, 148,* 1717-1720.

Ross, C. A., Miller, S., Reagor, P., Bjornson, L., Fraser, G. A., & Anderson, G. (1990). Structured interview data on 102 cases of multiple personality disorder from four centers. *Journal of Psychiatry, 147,* 596-601.

Ross, R. R., & McKay, H. B. (1979). *Self-mutilation.* Lexington, MA: Lexington.

Runtz, M. (1987). *The psychosocial adjustment of women who were sexually and physically abused during childhood and early adulthood: A focus on revictimization.* Unpublished master's thesis, University of Manitoba, Canada.

Runtz, M. (1991). *The influence of coping strategies and social support on recovery from child abuse.* Unpublished doctoral dissertation, University of Manitoba, Canada.

Runtz, M., & Briere, J. (1988). *Childhood sexual abuse, revictimization as an adult, and current symptomatology.* Paper presented at the National Symposium on Child Victimization, Anaheim, CA.

Russell, D. E. H. (1986). *The secret trauma: Incest in the lives of girls and women.* New York: Basic Books.

Sanders, B., & Giolas, M. H. (1991). Dissociation and childhood trauma in psychologically disturbed adolescents. *American Journal of Psychiatry, 148,* 50-54.

Sargant, W., & Slater, E. (1941). Amnestic syndromes of war. *Proceedings of the Royal Society of Medicine, 34,* 757-764.

Saunders, B. E., Mandoki, C., & Kilpatrick, D. G. (1989). *Development of a crime-related post-traumatic stress disorder scale within the Symptom Checklist 90 Revised.* Unpublished manuscript.

Scalzo, J. O. (1991). *Beyond survival: Keys to resilience among women who experienced childhood sexual abuse.* Unpublished doctoral dissertation, Simon Fraser University, Burnaby, British Columbia.

Schaef, A. W. (1986). *Co-dependence: Misunderstood—mistreated.* San Francisco: Harper & Row.

Schakel, J. A. (1987). Emotional neglect and stimulus deprivation. In M. R. Brassard, R. Germain, & S. N. Hart (Eds.), *Psychological maltreatment of children and youth* (pp. 100-109). New York: Pergamon.

Schneider-Rosen, K., & Cicchetti, D. (1984). The relationship between affect and cognition in maltreated infants: Quality of attachment and the development of visual self-recognition. *Child development, 55,* 648-658.

Schneidman, E. S. (1985). *Definition of suicide.* New York: John Wiley.

Sedlak, A. J. (1991). *National incidence and prevalence of child abuse and neglect: 1988* (rev. report). Rockville, MD: Westat.

Seligman, M. E. P. (1975). *Helplessness: On depression, development, and death.* San Francisco: Freeman.

Sgroi, S. M. (1989). *Vulnerable populations* (Vol. 1). Lexington, MA: Lexington.

Shukitt, M., Goodwin, D. W., & Winoker, G. (1972). A study of alcoholism in half-siblings. *American Journal of Psychiatry, 128,* 1132-1136.

Silbert, S. M., & Pines, A. M. (1981). Sexual child abuse as an antecedent to prostitution. *Child Abuse & Neglect, 5,* 407-411.

Smiljanich, K. (1992). *University students' self-reported sexual interest in children.* Unpublished master's thesis, California State University, Dominguez Hills.

Smiljanich, K., Briere, J., & Henschel, D. (1990, April). *Rape and consensual sexual fantasies in adults molested as children.* Paper presented at the annual meeting of the Western Psychological Association, Los Angeles.

Sonkin, D., Martin, D. J., & Walker, L. (1985). *The male batterer: A treatment approach.* New York: Springer.

Spiegel, D. (1989). Hypnosis in the treatment of victims of sexual abuse. *Psychiatric Clinics of North America: Treatment of Victims of Sexual Abuse, 12,* 295-305.

Spitz, R. (1945). Hospitalism: An inquiry into the genesis of psychiatric conditions in early childhood. *Psychoanalytic Study of the Child, 1,* 53-74.

Spitz, R. (1946). Anaclitic depression. *Psychoanalytic Study of the Child, 2,* 313-342.

Springs, F. E., & Friedrich, W. N. (in press). Health risk behaviors and medical sequelae of childhood sexual abuse. *Mayo Clinic Proceedings.*

Stacey, W. A., & Shupe, A. (1983). *The family secret: Domestic violence in America.* Boston: Beacon.

Steer, M. (1988, April). *A case presentation: An emerging history of abuse via the therapeutic process.* Paper presented at the First Annual Conference for Professionals Working With Adults Molested as Children, Portland, OR.

Steiger, H., & Zanko, M. (1990). Sexual traumata among eating disordered, psychiatric, and normal female groups: Comparison of prevalences and defense styles. *Journal of Interpersonal Violence, 5,* 74-86.

Stein, J. A., Golding, J. M., Siegel, J. M., Burnam, M. A., & Sorenson, S. B. (1988). Long-term psychological sequelae of child sexual abuse: The Los Angeles Epidemiologic Catchment Area Study. In G. E. Wyatt & G. J. Powell (Eds.), *Lasting effects of child sexual abuse* (pp. 135-154). Newbury Park, CA: Sage.

Stern, D. (1985). *The interpersonal world of the infant.* New York: Basic Books.

Stone, M. H. (1981). Borderline syndromes: A consideration of subtypes and overview, directions for research. *Psychiatric Clinics of North America, 4,* 3-13.

Stordeur, R. A., & Stille, R. (1989). *Ending men's violence against their partners: One road to peace.* Newbury Park, CA: Sage.

Straus, M., Gelles, R., & Steinmetz, S. (1980). *Behind closed doors: Violence in the American family.* Garden City, NY: Anchor/Doubleday.

Strober, M., & Humphrey, L. L. (1987). Familial contributions to the etiology and course of anorexia nervosa and bulimia. *Journal of Consulting and Clinical Psychology, 55,* 654-569.

Stukas-Davis, C. (1990). *The influence of childhood sexual abuse and male sex role socialization on adult sexual functioning.* Unpublished doctoral dissertation, California School of Professional Psychology, Los Angeles.

Summit, R. C. (1988). Hidden victims, hidden pain: Societal avoidance of child sexual abuse. In G. E. Wyatt & G. J. Powell (Eds.), *Lasting effects of child sexual abuse* (pp. 39-60). Newbury Park, CA: Sage.

Swett, C., Surrey, J., & Cohen, C. (1990). Sexual and physical abuse histories and psychiatric symptoms among male psychiatric outpatients. *American Journal of Psychiatry, 147,* 632-636.

Terr, L. (1990). *Too scared to cry: Psychic trauma in childhood.* New York: Harper & Row.

Trepper, T. S., & Barrett, M. J. (1989). *Systemic treatment of incest.* New York: Brunner/Mazel.

Urquiza, A., & Crowley, C. (1986, May). *Sex differences in the survivors of childhood sexual abuse.* Paper presented at the Fourth National Conference on the Sexual Victimization of Children, New Orleans.

van der Kolk, B. A. (1987). The psychological consequences of overwhelming life experience. In B. A. van der Kolk (Ed.), *Psychological trauma* (pp. 1-30). Washington, DC: American Psychiatric Press.

van der Kolk, B. A. (1989). The compulsion to repeat the trauma: Re-enactment, revictimization, and masochism. *Psychiatric Clinics of North America, 12,* 389-411.

van der Kolk, B. A., & Kadish, W. (1987). Amnesia, dissociation, and the return of the repressed. In B. A. van der Kolk (Ed.), *Psychological trauma* (pp. 173-190). Washington, DC: American Psychiatric Press.

van der Kolk, B. A., Perry, J. C., & Herman, J. L. (1991). Childhood origins of self-destructive behavior. *American Journal of Psychiatry, 148,* 1665 1671.

Vissing, Y. M., Straus, M. A., Gelles, R. J., & Harrop, J. W. (1991). Verbal aggression by parents and psychosocial problems of children. *Child Abuse & Neglect, 15,* 223-238.

Walker, E., Katon, W., Harrop-Griffiths, J., Holm, L., Russo, J., & Hickok, L. R. (1988). Relationship of chronic pelvic pain to psychiatric diagnosis and childhood sexual abuse. *American Journal of Psychiatry, 145,* 75-80.

Walsh, B. W., & Rosen, P. (1988) *Self-mutilation: Theory, research, and treatment.* New York: Guilford.

West, L. J. (1967). Dissociative reaction. In A. M. Freeman & H. I. Kaplan (Eds.), *Comprehensive textbook of psychiatry* (pp. 1544-1561). Baltimore: Williams & Wilkins.

Widom, C. S. (1989). The cycle of violence. *Science, 244,* 160-166.

Wiemers, K. S., & Petretic-Jackson, P. (1991, August). *Defining physical child abuse: Ratings of parental behaviors.* Paper presented at the annual meeting of the American Psychological Association, San Francisco.

Winoker, G., Cadoret, F., Dorzab, J., & Baker, M. (1971). Depressive disease: A genetic study. *Archives of General Psychiatry, 24,* 135-144.

Wyatt, G. E. (1985). The sexual abuse of Afro-American and white American women in childhood. *Child Abuse & Neglect, 9,* 231-240.

Wyatt, G. E., & Newcomb, M. (1991). Internal and external mediators of women's sexual abuse in childhood. *Journal of Consulting and Clinical Psychology, 58,* 758-767.

Zaidi, L. Y., Knutson, J. F., & Mehm, J. B. (1989). Transgenerational patterns of abusive parenting: Analogue and clinical tests. *Aggressive Behavior, 15,* 137-152.

Zivney, O. A., Nash, M. R., & Hulsey, T. L. (1988). Sexual abuse in early versus late childhood: Differing patterns of pathology as revealed on the Rorschach. *Psychotherapy, 25,* 99-106.

Index

About the Author

John N. Briere, Ph.D., is on faculty in the Department of Psychiatry and the Behavioral Sciences at the University of Southern California School of Medicine, and a clinical psychologist in the Department of Emergency Psychiatric Services of Los Angeles County-USC Medical Center. Specializing in psychological trauma, Dr. Briere speaks and writes on the topics of child abuse, victims of violence, and post-traumatic stress. He is on the editorial boards of several scholarly journals, and is a member of the Board of Directors of the American Professional Society on the Abuse of Children (APSAC). He is the author of *Therapy for Adults Molested as Children: Beyond Survival* (1989) and editor of the sourcebook *Treating Victims of Child Sexual Abuse* (1991).